Student Solutions Manual and Study Guide

for

Practical Business Math Procedures

Tenth Edition

Jeffrey Slater
North Shore Community College

Student Solutions Manual and Study Guide for
PRACTICAL BUSINESS MATH PROCEDURES
Jeffrey Slater

Published by McGraw-Hill/Irwin, an imprint of The McGraw-Hill Companies, Inc., 1221 Avenue of the
Americas, New York, NY 10020. Copyright © 2011, 2008, 2006, 2003, 2000, 1997, 1994, 1991, 1987, 1983 by The
McGraw-Hill Companies, Inc. All rights reserved.

1 2 3 4 5 6 7 8 9 0 WDQ/WDQ 1 0 9 8 7 6 5 4 3 2 1 0

ISBN: 978-0-07-732800-9
MHID: 0-07-732800-0

www.mhhe.com

Preface

This solutions booklet and study guide is intended a "back up" for your study by business math. The manual contain step-by-step solutions for an example or two of every kind of problem in the text. It also contains a student progress chart that lets you keep a record of your progress. Self-paced worksheets for each chapter are included, along with a Calculator Reference Guide.

Please realize that the worked out solutions should be used to help, not replace your effort at solving the problems. Here are a few tips to keep in mind while doing your assignments.

1. Put this Solutions Manual on another table where you can see it, but where you can't reach it. Then thin of trying to "beat it" by solving the problem without getting up to refer to it.

2. When you get to a tough problem and just can't quite solve it, go to another problem. Does it make sense? If not, go back and reread the problem.

3. If you are still stuck, try a guess and substitute the answer back into the problem. Does it seem logical? If not, go back and reread the problem remembering whether your guess was close or not.

4. Try looking at the example in the text that is similar to the problem. Does the method in the book give you any clues? Now look a the steps you wrote down in trying to solve the problem. How does it compare to the example?

5. When you do look up the solutions in this manual, cover the answer from the so that only the first line shows. Then look at the first step only. How does it compare to your first step? Then go down line by line.

6. Just stick with it. You'll do fine!

Contents

Student Progress Chart..vi

Chapter 1: Whole Numbers: How to Dissect and Solve Word Problems....................... 1

Chapter 2: Fractions...6

Chapter 3: Decimals..8

Chapter 4: Banking 10

Chapter 5: Solving for the Unknown: A How-To Approach for Solving Equations...................12

Chapter 6: Percents and Their Applications 15

Chapter 7: Discounts: Trade and Cash...19

Chapter 8: Markups and Markdowns: Perishables and Breakeven Analysis 22

Chapter 9: Payroll 26

Chapter 10: Simple Interest 29

Chapter 11: Promissory Notes, Simple-Discount Notes, and the Discount
            Process 32

Chapter 12: Compound Interest and Present Value..34

Chapter 13: Annuities and Sinking Funds 36

Chapter 14: Installment Buying, Rule of 78 and Revolving Charge Credit Cards.............39

Chapter 15: The Cost of Home Ownership..42

Chapter 16: How to Read, Analyze and Interpret Financial
            Reports 44

Chapter 17: Depreciation 47

Chapter 18: Inventory and Overhead...49

Chapter 19: Sales, Excise and Property Taxes..52

Chapter 20: Life, Fire and Auto Insurance 54

Chapter 21: Stocks, Bonds and Mutual Funds...56

Chapter 22: Business Statistics 58

Self-paced Worksheets...61

Calculator Reference Guide 120

STUDENT PROGRESS CHART

Chapter	LU	Title	Objectives reviewed	Practice quizzes completed	Review chapter** organizer with vocabulary and drill and word problems completed	Challenge problems completed	Summary practice test completed	Video and/or computer software reviewed	Additional set of drill and word problems by learning unit or cumulative review completed	Exam grade on chapter
1	1-1	Reading/Writing Whole Numbers								
	1-2	Addition/Subtraction								
	1-3	Multiplication/Division								
2	2-1	Fractions/Conversions								
	2-2	Fractions/Add/Sub								
	2-3	Fractions/Mult/Div								
3	3-1	Dec/Conversions/Rounding								
	3-2	Dec/Add/Sub/Mult/Div/Foreign Currency								
4	4-1	Checking Account								
	4-2	Bank Reconciliation								
5	5-1	Equations								
	5-2	Word Problems								
6	6-1	Percent/Conversions								
	6-2	Portion Formula								
7	7-1	Trade Discounts								
	7-2	Cash Discount/Credit Terms								
8	8-1	Markup-Cost								
	8-2	Markup-Selling Price								
	*8-3	Markdowns/Perishables								
	*8-4	Breakeven analysis								
9	9-1	Payroll-Gross								
	9-2	Payroll Deductions/Employer Responsibilities								
10	10-1	Simple Interest								
	10-2	Principal/Rate/Time								
	10-3	U.S. Rule								
11	11-1	Promissory/Simple Discount Note								
	11-2	Discounting								
12	12-1	Compound Interest								
	12-2	Present Value								
13	13-1	Annuities/Ordinary/Due								
	13-2	Present Value of Annuity								
	13-3	Sinking Fund								

*Not in Tenth Edition; **Self-paced learning worksheets in could be complete. vii

STUDENT PROGRESS CHART

Chapter	LU	Title	Objectives reviewed	Practice quizzes completed	Review chapter ** organizer with vocabulary and drill and word problems completed	Challenge problems completed	Summary practice test completed	Video and/or computer software reviewed	Additional set of drill and word problems by learning unit or cumulative review completed	Exam grade on chapter
14	14-1	Installment Buying								
	14-2	Rule of 78								
	14-3	Revolving Charge/Av. Daily Balance								
15	15-1	Monthly Payment								
	15-2	Amortization Schedule								
16	16-1	Balance Sheet								
	16-2	Income Statement								
	16-3	Trend/Ratio Analysis								
17	17-1	Concepts/Straight Line								
	17-2	Units-of-Production								
	17-3	Declining Balance								
	17-4	MACRS & ACRS								
	17-5	MACRS								
18	18-1	Sp. Id./Wtd. Av./FIFO/LIFO								
	18-2	Retail/Gross Profit/Turn/Overload								
19	19-1	Sales/Excise Tax								
	19-2	Property Tax								
20	20-1	Life Insurance								
	20-2	Fire Insurance								
	20-3	Auto Insurance								
21	21-1	Stocks								
	21-2	Bonds								
22	22-1	Mean/Median/Mode								
	22-2	Frequency Distribution/Graphs								
	22-3	Measures of Dispersion								

CHAPTER 1 – Whole Numbers: How to Dissect and Solve Word Problems

End–of-Chapter Problems

Drill Problems:

1-9.   Add the following:

```
   99
+  15
  114
```

1-19.   Multiply the following:

```
    450
×   280
 36 000
 90 0
126,000
```

1-23.   Divide the following by long division. Show work and remainder:

```
      86 R4
6)520
    48
    40
    36
     4
```

1-29.   Add the following and check by totaling each column individually without carrying numbers:

	Check
8,539	16
6,842	16
+ 9,495	17
24,876	23
	24,876

1-31.   Estimate the following by rounding all the way and then do actual addition:

Actual	Estimate
6,980	7,000
3,190	3,000
+ 7,819	+ 8,000
17,989	18,000

1

1-39. Divide the following and check by multiplication:

```
      19 R21
45)876              Check
  45              45 × 19 =  855
 426                     + 21 (R)
 405                       876
  21
```

1-41. Complete the following:

```
   9,200
 − 1,510
   7,690
 −   700
   6,990
```

1-43. Estimate the following problem by rounding all the way and ten do the actual multiplication:

```
 Actual          Estimate
   870              900
 ×  81            ×   80
   870            72,000
 69 60
 70,470
```

Word Problems:

1-49. Assume season-ticket prices in the lower bowl for the Buffalo Bills will rise from $480 for a 10-game package to $600. Fans sitting in the best seats in the upper deck will pay an increase from $440 to $540. Don Manning plans to purchase 2 season tickets for either lower bowl or upper deck. **(a)** How much more will 2 tickets cost for lower bowl? **(b)** How much more will 2 tickets cost for upper deck? **(c)** What will be his total cost for a 10-game package for lower bowl? **(d)** What will be his total cost for a 10-game package for upper deck?

a.
```
   $600
  −480
  $120 per ticket
  ×  2
  $240 for 2 tickets
```

b.
```
   $540
  −440
  $100 per ticket
  ×  2
  $200 for 2 tickets
```

c.
```
 $ 600
 ×   2
 $1,200
```

d.
```
 $ 540
 ×   2
 $1,080
```

1-53.   What was the total average number of visits for these Internet Web sites?

Web site	Average daily unique visitors
1. Orbitz.com	1,527,000
2. Mypoints.com	1,356,000
3. Americangreetings.com	745,000
4. Bizrate.com	503,000
5. Half.com	397,000

$$\begin{array}{r} 1,527,000 \\ 1,356,000 \\ 745,000 \\ 503,000 \\ +\ \ 397,000 \\ \hline 4,528,000 \text{ visitors} \end{array}$$

$$\begin{array}{r} 905,600 \text{ average} \\ 5\overline{)4,528,000} \\ 45 \\ \hline 28 \\ 25 \\ \hline 30 \\ 30 \\ \hline \end{array}$$

1-55.   A report from the Center for Science in the Public Interest—a consumer group based in Washington, DC—released a study listing calories of various ice cream treats sold by six of the largest ice cream companies. The worst treat tested by the group was 1,270 total calories. People need roughly 2,200 to 2,500 calories per day. Using a daily average, how many additional calories should a person consume after eating the ice cream?

$$\begin{array}{r} 2,200 \\ +2,500 \\ \hline 4,700 \end{array}$$

$$\begin{array}{r} 2,350 \text{ average} \\ 2\overline{)4,700} \\ 4 \\ \hline 7 \\ 6 \\ \hline 10 \\ 10 \\ \hline 0 \end{array}$$

$$\begin{array}{r} ^{2\ 15} \\ 2,\cancel{3}\cancel{5}0 \\ -\ 1,270 \\ \hline 1,080 \end{array}$$

1-57.   Lee Wills, professor of business, has 18 students in Accounting I, 26 in Accounting II, 22 in Introduction to Computers, 23 in Business Law, and 29 in Introduction to Business. What is the total number of students in Professor Wills's classes? If 12 students withdraw, how many total students will Professor Wills have?

$$\begin{array}{l} 118\ (18 + 26 + 22 + 23 + 29) \\ -\ 12 \\ \hline 106 \text{ students} \end{array}$$

1-63.   Hometown Buffet had 90 customers on Sunday, 70 on Monday, 65 on Tuesday, and a total of 310 on Wednesday to Saturday. How many customers did Hometown Buffet serve during the week? If each customer spends $9, what were the total sales for the week?

$$90 + 70 + 65 + 310 = \quad 535 \text{ customers}$$
$$\times \quad \$9$$
$$\overline{\$4,815}$$

If Hometown Buffet had the same sales each week, what were the sales for the year?

$$\$4,815 \times 52 = \$250,380$$

1-73.   While redecorating, Lee Owens went to Carpet World and bought 150 square yards of commercial carpet. The total cost of the carpet was $6,000. How much did Lee pay per square yard?

$$\$6,000 \div 150 = \$40 \text{ per square yard}$$

Challenge Problem:

1-76.   Paula Sanchez is trying to determine her 2011 finances. Paula's actual 2010 finances were as follows:

Income:		Assets:		
Gross income	$69,000	Checking account	$ 1,950	
Interest income	450	Savings account	8,950	
Total	$69,450	Automobile	1,800	
Expenses:		Personal property	14,000	
Living	$24,500	Total	$26,700	
Insurance premium	350	Liabilities:		
Taxes	14,800	Note to bank	4,500	
Medical	585	Net worth	$22,200	($26,700 − $4,500)
Investment	4,000			
Total	$44,235			

Net worth = Assets − Liabilities

(own)   (owe)

4

Paula believes her gross income will double in 2011 but her interest income will decrease $150. She plans to reduce her 2011 living expenses by one-half. Paula's insurance company wrote a letter announcing that her insurance premiums would triple in 2011. Her accountant estimates her taxes will decrease $250 and her medical costs will increase $410. Paula also hopes to cut her investments expenses by one-fourth. Paula's accountant projects that her savings and checking accounts will each double in value. On January 2, 2011, Paula sold her automobile and began to use public transportation. Paula forecasts that her personal property will decrease by one-seventh. She has sent her bank a $375 check to reduce her bank note. Could you give Paula an updated list of her 2011 finances? If you round all the way each 2010 and 2011 asset and liability, what will be the difference in Paula's net worth?

Income:				Assets:		
Gross income	$138,000	($69,000 × 2)		Checking account	$ 3,900	($1,950 × 2)
Interest income	300	($450 − $150)		Savings account	17,900	($8,950 × 2)
Total	$138,300			Personal property	12,000	($14,000 − $\frac{1}{7}$ of $14,000)
Expenses:				Total	$33,800	
Living	$ 12,250	($24,500 ÷ 2)		Liabilities:		
Insurance premium	1,050	($350 × 3)		Note to bank	4,125	($4,500 − $375)
Taxes	14,550	($14,800 − $250)		Net worth	$29,675	
Medical	995	($585 + $410)				
Investment	3,000	($4,000 − $\frac{1}{4}$ of $4,000)				
Total	$ 31,845					

	2010	2011	
Checking account	$ 2,000	$ 4,000	
Savings account	9,000	20,000	
Automobile	2,000	0	
Personal property	10,000	10,000	
Total	$ 23,000	$34,000	$30,000 = 2011
Liabilities	5,000	4,000	− 18,000 = 2010
Net worth	$ 18,000	$30,000	$12,000

Total estimated difference is $12,000 in favor of 2011.

CHAPTER 2 – Fractions

End–of–Chapter problems

Drill problems:

2-3.   Identify the following types of fractions:

$$\frac{3}{7} \quad \text{Proper}$$

2-5.   Convert the following to mixed numbers:

$$\frac{921}{15} = 61\frac{6}{15} = 61\frac{2}{5}$$

2-9.   Reduce the following to the lowest terms. Show how to calculate the greatest common divisor by the step approach.

$$\frac{44}{52} = \frac{44 \div 4}{52 \div 4} = \frac{11}{13}$$

$$\begin{array}{ccc}
1 & 5 & 2 \\
44\overline{)52} & 8\overline{)44} & 4\overline{)8} \\
\underline{44} & \underline{40} & \underline{8} \\
8 & 4 & 0
\end{array}$$

2-13.   Determine the LCD of the following (a) by inspection and (b) by division of prime numbers:

$$\frac{1}{4}, \frac{3}{32}, \frac{5}{48}, \frac{1}{8}$$

Inspection 96
$2 \times 2 \times 2 \times 2 \times 2 \times 3 = 96$

Check

$$\begin{array}{c|cccc}
2 & 4 & 32 & 48 & 8 \\
2 & 2 & 16 & 24 & 4 \\
2 & 1 & 8 & 12 & 2 \\
2 & 1 & 4 & 6 & 1 \\
\hline
 & 1 & 2 & 3 & 1
\end{array}$$

2-21.   Subtract the following and reduce to lowest terms.

$$12\frac{1}{9} - 4\frac{2}{3} \qquad 12\frac{1}{9} = 11\frac{10}{9} \left(\frac{9}{9} + \frac{1}{9} \right)$$

$$\begin{array}{r}
-4\frac{6}{9} = -4\frac{6}{9} \\
\hline
7\frac{4}{9}
\end{array}$$

2-25.   Multiply the following. Use the cancellation technique.

$$\frac{4}{10} \times \frac{30}{60} \times \frac{6}{10} = \frac{\overset{1}{\cancel{4}}}{\underset{5}{\cancel{10}}} \times \frac{\overset{3}{\cancel{30}}}{\underset{5}{\cancel{60}}} \times \frac{\overset{1}{\cancel{6}}}{\underset{1}{\cancel{10}}} = \frac{3}{25}$$

Word Problems:

2-33. Britney Summers visited Curves and lost $2\frac{1}{4}$ pounds in week 1, $1\frac{3}{4}$ pounds in week 2, and $\frac{5}{8}$ pound in week 3. What is the total weight loss for Britney?

$$2\frac{2}{8} + 1\frac{6}{8} + \frac{5}{8} = 3\frac{13}{8} = 4\frac{5}{8} \text{ pounds}$$

2-37. Tiffani Lind got her new weekly course schedule from Roxbury Community College in Boston. Following are her classes and their length: Business Math-$2\frac{1}{2}$ hours, Introduction to Business-$1\frac{1}{2}$ hours, Microeconomics-$1\frac{1}{2}$ hours, Spanish-$2\frac{1}{4}$ hours, Marketing-$1\frac{1}{4}$ hours and Business Statistics-$1\frac{3}{4}$ hours long. How long will she be in class each week?

$$2\frac{1}{2} + 1\frac{1}{2} + 1\frac{1}{2} + 2\frac{1}{4} + 1\frac{1}{4} + 1\frac{3}{4} =$$

$$2\frac{2}{4} + 1\frac{2}{4} + 1\frac{2}{4} + 2\frac{1}{4} + 1\frac{1}{4} + 1\frac{3}{4} = 8\frac{11}{4} = 10\frac{3}{4} \text{ hours in class each week}$$

2-43. Marc, Steven, and Daniel entered into a Subway sandwich shop partnership. Marc owns $\frac{1}{9}$ of the shop and Steven owns $\frac{1}{4}$. What part does Daniel own?

$$\frac{4}{36} + \frac{9}{36} = \frac{13}{36} \qquad 1 - \frac{13}{36} = \frac{23}{36} \text{ for Daniel or } \frac{36}{36} - \frac{13}{36} = \frac{23}{36}$$

2-45. Hertz pays Al Davis, an employee, \$125 per day. Al decides to donate $\frac{1}{5}$ of a day's pay to his church. How much will Al donate?

$$\frac{1}{5} \times \$125 = \$25$$

2-51. Tempco Corporation has a machine that produces $12\frac{1}{2}$ baseball gloves each hour. In the last 2 days, the machine has run for a total of 22 hours. How many baseball gloves has Tempco produced?

$$22 \times 12\frac{1}{2} = \overset{11}{22} \times \frac{25}{\underset{1}{2}} = 275 \text{ gloves}$$

2-55. An issue of *Taunton's Fine Woodworking* included plans for a hall stand. The total height of the stand is $81\frac{1}{2}$ inches. If the base is $36\frac{5}{16}$ inches, how tall is the upper portion of the stand?

$$
\begin{aligned}
81\frac{1}{2} &= \quad 81\frac{8}{16}\\
-\,36\frac{5}{16} &= -\,36\frac{5}{16}\\
\hline
&\quad\ \ 45\frac{3}{16} \text{ inches}
\end{aligned}
$$

Additional Set of Word Problems:

2-59. Tamara, Jose, and Milton entered into a partnership that sells men's clothing on the Web. Tamara owns $\frac{3}{8}$ of the company, and Jose owns $\frac{1}{4}$. What part does Milton own?

$$\frac{3}{8} + \frac{2}{8} = \frac{5}{8} \qquad 1 - \frac{5}{8} = \frac{3}{8} \text{ for Milton or } \frac{8}{8} - \frac{5}{8} = \frac{3}{8}$$

CHAPTER 3 – Decimals

End–of–Chapter Problems

Drill problems:

3-3.   Round the following as indicated:

	Tenth	Hundredth	Thousandth
.8466	.8	.85	.847

3-17.   Convert the following types of decimal fractions to decimals (round to nearest hundredth as needed):

$16\dfrac{61}{100}$ 16.61

Word Problems:

3-33.   Rearrange the following and add:

.115,   10.8318,   4.7,   802.4811   818.1279

3-51.   Convert the following to decimals and round to the nearest hundredth:

$\dfrac{5}{8}$ .63

3-67.   The stock of Intel has a high of $30.25 today. It closed at $28.85. How much did the stock drop from its high?

$$\begin{array}{r} \overset{9\ 12}{\$3\cancel{0}.25} \\ -\ 28.85 \\ \hline \$\ 1.40 \end{array}$$

3-71.   Bob Ross bought a Blackberry on the Web for $89.99. He saw the same Blackberry in the mall for $118.99. How much did Bob save by buying on the Web?

$$\begin{array}{r} \overset{10\ 18}{\$1\cancel{1}8.99} \\ -\ 89.99 \\ \hline \$\ 29.00 \end{array}$$

3-77.   Roger bought season tickets for weekend games to professional basketball games. The cost was $945.60. The season package included 36 home games. What is the average price of the tickets per game? Round to the nearest cent. Marcelo, Roger's friend, offered to buy 4 of the tickets from Roger. What is the total amount Roger should receive?

$945.60 ÷ 36 = $26.27

$$\begin{array}{r} \$\ 26.27 \\ \times\qquad 4 \\ \hline \$105.08 \end{array}$$

Additional Set of Word Problems:

3-81. Tie Yang bought season tickets to the Boston Pops for $698.55. The season package included 38 performances. What is the average price of the tickets per performance? Round to nearest cent. Sam, Tie's friend, offered to buy 4 of the tickets from Tie. What is the total amount Tie should receive?

$698.55 ÷ 38 = $18.38 × 4 = $73.52

3-83. The *Denver Post* reported that Xcel Energy is revising customer charges for monthly residential electric bills and gas bills. Electric bills will increase $3.32. Gas bills will decrease $1.74 a month. (a) What is the resulting new monthly increase for the entire bill? (b) If Xcel serves 2,350 homes, how much additional revenue would Xcel receive each month?

a. $3.32
  − 1.74
  ───────
  $1.58 increase

b.   2,350
   × $1.58
   ─────────
   $3,713.00

Challenge Problem:

3-87. Jill and Frank decided to take a long weekend in New York. City Hotel has a special getaway weekend for $79.95. The price is per person per night, based on double occupancy. The hotel has a minimum two-night stay. For this price, Jill and Frank will receive $50 credit toward their dinners at City's Skylight Restaurant. Also included in the package is a $3.99 credit per person toward breakfast for two each morning.

Since Jill and Frank do not own a car, they plan to rent a car. The car rental agency charges $19.95 a day with an additional charge of $.22 a mile and $1.19 per gallon of gas used. The gas tank holds 24 gallons.

From the following facts, calculate the total expenses of Jill and Frank (round all answers to nearest hundredth or cent as appropriate). Assume no taxes.

Car rental (2 days):		Dinner cost at Skylight	$182.12
Beginning odometer reading	4,820	Breakfast for two:	
Ending odometer reading	4,940	Morning No. 1	24.17
Beginning gas tank: $\frac{3}{4}$ full.		Morning No. 2	26.88
Gas tank on return: $\frac{1}{2}$ full.			
Tank holds 24 gallons.			

$79.95 × 2 = $159.90 × 2   = $319.80

$182.12
− 50.00   132.12
─────────
$132.12

                $24.17
Breakfast No. 1: − 7.98   16.19
                ───────
                $16.19

                $26.88
Breakfast No. 2: − 7.98   18.90
                ───────
                $18.90

2 × $19.95   39.90

$.22 × 120 (4,940 − 4,820)   26.40

$\frac{1}{4}$ × 24 = 6 gallons × $1.19   7.14
                                 ─────────
                                 $560.45

CHAPTER 4 – Banking

End–of–Chapter Problems

Drill problems:

4-1.   Fill out the check register that follows with this information:

2010
July 7	Check No. 482	AOL	$143.50
15	Check No. 483	Staples	66.10
19	Deposit		800.00
20	Check No. 484	Sprint	451.88
24	Check No. 485	Krispy Kreme	319.24
29	Deposit		400.30

		RECORD ALL CHARGES OR CREDITS THAT AFFECT YOUR ACCOUNT						
NUMBER	DATE 2009	DESCRIPTION OF TRANSACTION	PAYMENT/DEBIT (−)	√	FEE (IF ANY) (−)	DEPOSIT/CREDIT (+)	BALANCE	
							$ 4,500	75
482	7/7	AOL	$ 143 50		$	$	− 143	50
							4,357	25
483	7/15	Staples	66 10				− 66	10
							4,291	15
	7/19	Deposit				800 00	+ 800	00
							5,091	15
484	7/20	Sprint	451 88				− 451	88
							4,639	27
485	7/24	Krispy Kreme	319 24				− 319	24
							4,320	03
	7/29	Deposit				400 30	+ 400	30
							$4,720	33

4-3.   Using the check register in Problem 4–1 and the following bank statement, prepare a bank reconciliation for Lee.com.

BANK STATEMENT			
Date	Checks	Deposits	Balance
7/1 balance			$4,500.75
7/18	$143.50		4,357.25
7/19		$ 800.00	5,157.25
7/26	319.24		4,838.81
7/30	15.00 SC		4,823.01

Lee.com checkbook balance	$4,720.33	Bank balance		$4,823.01
		Add:		
		Deposit in transit		400.30
Deduct:		Deduct:		
Service charge	15.00	Outstanding checks:		
		No. 483	$ 66.10	
		No. 484	451.88	517.98
Ending checkbook balance	$4,705.33	Ending bank balance		$4,705.33

Word Problems:

4-9. Banks are finding more ways to charge fees, such as a $25 overdraft fee. Sue McVickers has an account in Fayetteville; she has received her bank statement with this $25 charge. Also, she was charged a $6.50 service fee; however, the good news is she earned $5.15 interest. Her bank statement's balance was $315.65, but it did not show the $1,215.15 deposit she had made. Sue's checkbook balance shows $604.30. The following checks have not cleared: No. 250, $603.15; No. 253, $218.90; and No. 254, $130.80. Prepare Sue's bank reconciliation.

Sue's checkbook balance		$604.30	Bank balance		$ 315.65
Add:			Add:		
Interest		5.15	Deposit in transit		1,215.15
		$609.45			$1,530.80
Deduct:			Deduct:		
Service charge	$ 6.50		Outstanding checks:		
Overdraft	25.00	31.50	No. 250	$603.15	
			No. 253	218.90	
			No. 254	130.80	952.85
Reconciled balance		$577.95	Reconciled balance		$ 577.95

4-11. Lowell Bank reported the following checking account fees: $2 to see a real-live teller, $20 to process a bounced check, and $1 to $3 if you need an original check to prove you paid a bill or made a charitable contribution. This past month you had to transact business through a teller 6 times—a total $12 cost to you. Your bank statement shows a $305.33 balance; your checkbook shows a $1,009.76 balance. You received $1.10 in interest. An $801.15 deposit was not recorded on your statement. The following checks were outstanding: No. 413, $28.30; No. 414, $18.60; and No. 418, $60.72. Prepare your bank reconciliation.

Checkbook balance		$1,009.76	Bank balance		$ 305.33
Add:			Add:		
Interest		1.10	Deposit in transit		801.15
		$1,010.86			$1,106.48
Deduct:			Deduct:		
Teller fee		12.00	Outstanding checks:		
			No. 413	$28.30	
			No. 414	18.60	
			No. 418	60.72	107.62
Reconciled balance		$ 998.86	Reconciled balance		$ 998.86

CHAPTER 5 – Solving for the Unknown: A How-To Approach for Solving Equations

End–of–Chapter Problems

Drill Problems (First of Three Sets):

5-1.   Solve the unknown from the following equations:

$$\begin{array}{r} E - 20 = 110 \\ +20 \quad\ +20 \\ \hline E \quad = 130 \end{array}$$

5-5. $5Y = 75$

$$\frac{5Y}{5} = \frac{75}{5}$$
$$Y = 15$$

5-9. $4(P - 9) = 64$

$$\begin{array}{r} 4P - 36 = 64 \\ +36 \quad +36 \\ \hline \dfrac{4P}{4} = \dfrac{100}{4} \\ P = 25 \end{array}$$

Word Problems (First of Three Sets):

5-11.   Kathy and Jeanne are elementary school teachers. Jeanne works for Marquez Charter School in Pacific Palisades, California, where class size reduction is a goal for 2009. Kathy works for a noncharter school where funds do not allow for class size reduction policies. Kathy's fifth-grade class has 1.5 times as many students as Jeanne's. If there are a total of 60 students, how many students does Jeanne's class have? How many students does Kathy's class have?

Unknown(s)	Variable(s)	Relationship
Kathy	1.5X	1.5X
Jeanne	X	+ X
		60 total students

$$X + 1.5X = 60$$
$$2.5X = 60$$
$$X = 24 \text{ (Jeanne)}$$
$$1.5X = 36 \text{ (Kathy)}$$

5-13.   Joe Sullivan and Hugh Kee sell cars for a Ford dealer. Over the past year, they sold 300 cars. Joe sells 5 times as many cars as Hugh. How many cars did each sell?

Unknown(s)	Variable(s)	Relationship
Hugh	C	C
Joe	5C	+5C
		300 cars

$$5C + C = 300$$
$$\frac{6C}{6} = \frac{300}{6}$$
$$C = 50$$
$$C = 50 \text{ (Hugh)}$$
$$5C = 250 \text{ (Joe)}$$

5-15. Dots sells T-shirts ($2) and shorts ($4). In April, total sales were $600. People bought 4 times as many T-shirts as shorts. How many T-shirts and shorts did Dots sell? Check your answer.

Unknown(s)	Variable(s)	Price	Relationship
T-shirts	4S	$2	8S
Shorts	S	4	+ 4S
			$600 total sales

$$8S + 4S = 600$$
$$\frac{\cancel{12}S}{\cancel{12}} = \frac{600}{12}$$
$$S = 50 \text{ shorts}$$
$$4S = 200 \text{ T-shirts}$$

Check
$$50(\$4) + 200(\$2) = \$600$$
$$\$200 + \$400 = \$600$$
$$\$600 = \$600$$

Drill Problems (Second of Three Sets):

5-17.
$$7B = 490$$
$$\frac{\cancel{7}B}{\cancel{7}} = \frac{490}{7}$$
$$B = 70$$

Word Problems (Second of Three Sets):

5-23. On a flight from Boston to San Diego, American reduced its Internet price by $190.00. The sale price was $420.99. What was the original price?

Unknown(s)	Variable(s)	Relationship
Original price	P	P − $190.00 = Sale price Sale price = $420.99

$$
\begin{array}{ll}
P - \$190 = & \$420.99 \\
+\ 190 & +\ 190.00 \\
\hline
P = & \$610.99
\end{array}
$$

5-25. Bill's Roast Beef sells 5 times as many sandwiches as Pete's Deli. The difference between their sales is 360 sandwiches. How many sandwiches did each sell?

Unknown(s)	Variable(s)	Relationship
Bill's	5S	5S (450)
Pete's	S	− S (90)
		360 sandwiches

$$5S - S = 360$$
$$\frac{\cancel{4}S}{\cancel{4}} = \frac{360}{4}$$
$$S = 90 \text{ (Pete's)}$$
$$5S = 450 \text{ (Bill's)}$$

Drill Problems (Third of Three Sets):

5-29.
$$
\begin{array}{ll}
A + 90 - 15 = & 210 \\
A + 75 = & 210 \\
-\ 75 & -\ 75 \\
\hline
A = & 135
\end{array}
$$

5-31.
$$
\begin{array}{ll}
3M + 20 = & 2M + 80 \\
-\ 2M & = -2M \\
\hline
M + 20 = & +\ 80 \\
-\ 20 & -\ 20 \\
\hline
M = & 60
\end{array}
$$

Word Problems (Third of Three Sets):

5-33. In 2008, FDNY, New York City Fire Department, had 221 fire houses with 11,275 full-time uniformed firefighters. During 2008, they responded to a total of 473,335 incidents. The top five engine companies responded to an average of 5,254 calls. Engine 75 had a total of 18 calls in one 24-hour shift. They responded to five times as many medical emergencies as they did structural fires. How many structural fires did they respond to in that 24-hour shift?

Unknown(s)	Variable(s)	Relationship
Med. emerg.	$5X$	$5X$
Structural fires	X	$\underline{+ X}$
		18 calls

Medical emergencies $= 5X$
Structural fires $= X$

$$5X + X = 18$$
$$6X = 18$$
$$X = 3$$
$$5X = 15$$

5-39. Ace Hardware sells boxes of wrenches ($100) and hammers ($300). Howard ordered 40 boxes of wrenches and hammers for $8,400. How many boxes of each are in the order? Check your answer.

Unknown(s)	Variable(s)	Price	Relationship
Wrenches	$40 - H$	$100	$100(40 - H)$
Hammers	H	300	$+ 300H$
			Total = $8,400

$$300H + 100(40 - H) = 8,400$$
$$300H + 4,000 - 100H = 8,400$$
$$200H + 4,000 = 8,400$$
$$\underline{- 4,000} \qquad \underline{- 4,000}$$
$$\frac{200H}{200} = \frac{4,400}{200}$$
$$H = 22 \text{ boxes of hammers}$$
$$40 - H = 18 \text{ boxes of wrenches}$$

Check
$$22(\$300) + 18(\$100) = \$8,400$$
$$\$6,600 + \$1,800 = \$8,400$$
$$\$8,400 = \$8,400$$

Challenge Problem:

5-41. Bessy has 6 times as much money as Bob, but when each earns $6, Bessy will have 3 times as much money as Bob. How much does each have before and after earning the $6?

Unknown(s)	Variable(s)	Relationship
Bessy	$6B$	$6B + 6$
Bob	B	$B + 6$

$$6B + 6 = 3(B + 6)$$
$$6B + 6 = 3B + 18$$
$$\underline{- 3B} \qquad \underline{- 3B}$$
$$3B + 6 = 18$$
$$\underline{- 6} \qquad \underline{- 6}$$
$$\frac{3B}{3} = \frac{12}{3}$$
$$B = 4$$

Before: $B = 4$ After: $B = 10$
$6B = 24$ $6B = 30$

CHAPTER 6 – Percents and Their Applications

End–of–Chapter Problems

Drill Problems:

6-5.   Convert the following decimals to percents:

3.561 356.1%

6-9.   Convert the following percents to decimals:

$64\frac{3}{10}\%$ .643

6-13.   Convert the following fractions to percents (round to the nearest tenth percent as needed):

$\frac{1}{12} = .0833 = 8.3\%$

6-17.   Convert the following to fractions and reduce to the lowest terms:

4% $4 \times \frac{1}{100} = \frac{4}{100} = \frac{1}{25}$

6-19. $31\frac{2}{3}\%$ $\frac{95}{3} \times \frac{1}{100} = \frac{95}{300} = \frac{19}{60}$

6-27.   Solve for the portion (round to the nearest hundredth as needed) $P = R^{x} B$:

17.4% of 900
■ .174 × 900 = 156.6

6-31.   18% of 90
.18 × 90 = 16.2

Solve for the base (round to the nearest hundredth as needed): $\frac{P}{R} = B$

6-33.   170 is 120% of ___141.67___ $\left(\frac{170}{1.2}\right)$

6-37. 800 is $4\frac{1}{2}$% of __17,777.78__ $\left(\dfrac{800}{.045}\right)$

6-41. Solve for rate (round to the nearest tenth percent as needed): $\dfrac{P}{B} = R$

110 is __110%__ of 100 $\left(\dfrac{110}{100}\right)$

6-43. 16 is __400%__ of 4 $\left(\dfrac{16}{4}\right)$

Solve the following problems. Be sure to show your work. Round to the nearest hundredth or hundredth percent as needed.

6-47. 770 is 70% of what number? $\qquad \dfrac{770}{.7} = 1,100 \qquad \dfrac{P}{R} = B$

6-49. What percent of 150 is 60? $\qquad \dfrac{60}{150} = 40\% \qquad \dfrac{P}{B} = R$

6-51. Complete the following table:

Product	Selling price		Amount of decrease or increase	Percent change (to nearest hundredth percent as needed)
	2008	2009		
College textbook	$100	$120	+$20	+20% $\left(\dfrac{\$20}{\$100}\right)$

Word Problems (First of Three Sets):

6-53. What percent of customers in Problem 6–52 did not order coffee?
$\dfrac{960}{1,200} = 80\%$

Note: Portion and rate must refer to same piece of the base.

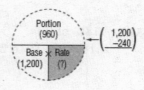

6-57. Jeff Rowe went to Best Buy and bought a Canon digital camera. The purchase price was $400. Jeff made a down payment of 40%. How much was Jeff's down payment?
.40 × $400 = $160

6-61. Out of 9,000 college students surveyed, 540 responded that they do not eat breakfast. What percent of the students do not eat breakfast?

$$\frac{540}{9,000} = .06 = 6\%$$

Note: Portion is smaller than base since rate is less than 100%.

Word Problems (Second of Three Sets):

6-63. Alice Hall made a $3,000 down payment on a new Ford Explorer wagon. She still owes 90% of the selling price. What was the selling price of the wagon?

$$\frac{\$3,000}{.10} = \$30,000$$

6-65. Jim and Alice Lange, employees at Walmart, have put themselves on a strict budget. Their goal at year's end is to buy a boat for $15,000 in cash. Their budget includes the following:

40% food and lodging   20% entertainment   10% educational

Jim earns $1,900 per month and Alice earns $2,400 per month. After one year, will Alice and Jim have enough cash to buy the boat?

100% − 40% − 20% − 10% = 30%

$1,900 × 12 = $22,800
$2,400 × 12 = $28,800
                    $51,600 × .30 = $15,480   Yes.

6-71. Dr. Grossman was reviewing his total accounts receivable. This month, credit customers paid $44,000, which represented 20% of all receivables (what customers owe) due. What was Dr. Grossman's total accounts receivable?

$$\frac{\$44,000}{.20} = \$220,000$$

Word Problems (Third of Three Sets):

6-77. In 2011, Jim Goodman, an employee at Walgreens, earned $45,900, an increase of 17.5% over the previous year. What were Jim's earnings in 2010? Round to the nearest cent.

$$B = \frac{\$45,900}{1.175} = \$39,063.83$$

6-81.   Earl Miller, a lawyer, charges Lee's Plumbing, his client, 25% of what he can collect for Lee from customers whose accounts are past due. The attorney also charges, in addition to the 25%, a flat fee of $50 per customer. This month, Earl collected $7,000 from 3 of Lee's past-due customers. What is the total fee due to Earl?

$$\$7,000 \times .25 = \$1,750$$
$$3 \times \$50 = \underline{\quad 150}$$
$$\$1,900$$

6-83.   Blockbuster Video uses MasterCard. MasterCard charges $2\frac{1}{2}\%$ on net deposits (credit slips less returns). Blockbuster made a net deposit of $4,100 for charge sales. How much did MasterCard charge Blockbuster?

$$\$4,100 \times .025 = \$102.50$$

6-89.   Jay Miller sold his ski house at Attitash Mountain in New Hampshire for $35,000. This sale represented a loss of 15% off the original price. What was the original price Jay paid for the ski house? Round your answer to the nearest dollar.

$$\frac{\$35,000}{.85} = \$41,176$$

6-93.   Assume 450,000 people line up on the streets to see the Macy's Thanksgiving Parade in 2010. If attendance is expected to increase 30%, what will be the number of people lined up on the street to see the 2011 parade?

$$450,000 \times 1.30 = 585,000$$

6-95.   A local Dunkin' Donuts shop reported that its sales have increased exactly 22% per year for the last 2 years. This year's sales were $82,500. What were Dunkin' Donuts sales 2 years ago? Round each year's sales to the nearest dollar.

$$\frac{\$82,500}{1.22} = \$67,623 \text{ sales last year} \qquad \frac{\$67,623}{1.22} = \$55,429$$

CHAPTER 7 – Discounts: Trade and Cash

End–of–Chapter Problems

Drill Problems:

For all the problems, round your final answer to the nearest cent. Do not round net price equivalent rates or single equivalent discount rates.

7-1.   Complete the following:

Item	List price	Chain discount	Net price equivalent rate (in decimals)	Single equivalent discount rate (in decimals)	Trade discount	Net price
Verizon Blackberry	$299	4/1	.9504	.0496	$14.83	$284.17

$$\begin{array}{cc} 1.00 & 1.00 \\ -\ .04 & -\ .01 \\ \hline .96\ \times & .99 \end{array} = .9504 \times \$299 = \$284.17$$

$$\begin{array}{c} 1.0000 \\ -\ .9504 \\ \hline .0496 \end{array} \times \$299 = \$14.83$$

7-5.   Complete the following:

Item	List price	Chain discount	Net price	Trade discount
Maytag dishwasher	$450	8/5/6	$369.70	$80.30

$450 \times .82156 = \$369.70\ (.82156 = .92 \times .95 \times .94)$
$450 \times .17844 = \$80.30\ (1 - .82156 = .17844)$

7-7. | Land Rover roofrack | $1,850 | 12/9/6 | $1,392.59 | $457.41 |

$1,850 \times .752752 = \$1,392.59\ (.752752 = .88 \times .91 \times .94)$
$1,850 \times .247248 = \$457.41\ (1 - .752752 = .247248)$

7-9.

Invoice	Dates when goods received	Terms	Last day* of discount period	Final day bill is due (end of credit period)
June 18		1/10, n/30	June 28	July 18

By Table 7.1, June 18 = 169 + 30 = 199 ⟶ Search in Table 7.1.

7-13. | June 12 | | 3/10 EOM | July 10 | July 30 Discount and credit period begin at end of month of sale. |

7-15. Complete the following by calculating the cash discount and net amount paid:

Gross amount of invoice (freight charge already included)	Freight charge	Date of invoice	Terms of invoice	Date of payment	Cash discount	Net amount paid
$7,000	$100	4/8	2/10, n/60	4/15	$138 (.02 × $6,900)	$6,862 ($6,900 × .98 = $6,762 + $100 = $6,862)

7-19. Complete the following:

Amount of invoice	Terms	Invoice date	Actual partial payment made	Date of partial payment	Amount of payment to be credited	Balance outstanding
$700	2/10, n/60	5/6	$400	5/15	$408.16	$291.84

$$\frac{\$400}{.98} = \begin{array}{r} \$700.00 \\ - \ 408.16 \\ \hline \$291.84 \end{array}$$

Word Problems (Round to Nearest Cent as Needed):

7-21. The list price of an orange dial Luminox watch is $650. Katz Jewelers receives a trade discount of 30%. Find the trade discount amount and the net price.
$650 × .30 = $195
$650 × .70 = $455

7-25. A manufacturer of skateboards offered a 5/2/1 chain discount to many customers. Bob's Sporting Goods ordered 20 skateboards for a total $625 list price. What was the net price of the skateboards? What was the trade discount amount?

Net price   Trade discount
.95 × .98 × .99 = .92169 × $625 = $576.05625   .07831 × $625 = $48.94
= $576.06

7-29. Macy of New York sold LeeCo. of Chicago office equipment with a $6,000 list price. Sale terms were 3/10, n/30 FOB New York. Macy agreed to prepay the $30 freight. LeeCo. pays the invoice within the discount period. What does LeeCo. pay Macy?
.97 × $6,000 = $5,820 + $30 freight = $5,850

7-33. On August 1, Intel Corporation (Problem 7–32) returns $100 of the machinery due to defects. What does Intel pay Bally on August 5? Round to nearest cent.
$14,000
−   100 returns $8,340 × .98 = $8,173.20
$13,900 × .60 = $8,340

Additional Set of Word Problems:

7-39. Vail Ski Shop received a $1,201 invoice dated July 8 with 2/10, 1/15, n/60 terms. On July 22, Vail sent a $485 partial payment. What credit should Vail receive? What is Vail's outstanding balance?

$$\frac{\$485}{.99} = \$489.90$$

$$\begin{array}{r} \$1,201.00 \\ -\ 489.90 \\ \hline \$\ \ 711.10 \text{ balance outstanding} \end{array}$$

7-41. True Value received an invoice dated 4/15/02. The invoice had a $5,500 balance that included $300 freight. Terms were 4/10, 3/30, n/60. True Value pays the invoice on April 29. What amount does True Value pay?

$5,500 - $300 = $5,200 \times .97 = $5,044

$$\begin{array}{r} \$5,044 \\ +\ \ \ 300 \\ \hline \$5,344 \end{array}$$

7-43. Sam's Ski Boards.com offers 5/4/1 chain discounts to many of its customers. The Ski Hut ordered 20 ski boards with a total list price of $1,200. What is the net price of the ski boards? What was the trade discount amount? Round to the nearest cent.

$.95 \times .96 \times .99 = .90288$

$$\begin{array}{r} \$\ \ \ 1,200 \\ \times\ \ \ .90288 \\ \hline \$1,083.46 \text{ net price} \end{array}$$
$$\begin{array}{r} \$\ \ 1,200 \\ \times\ \ .09712\ (1 - .90288) \\ \hline \$116.54 \text{ trade discount} \end{array}$$

Challenge Problem:

7-49. On March 30, Century Television received an invoice dated March 28 from ACME Manufacturing for 50 televisions at a cost of $125 each. Century received a 10/4/2 chain discount. Shipping terms were FOB shipping point. ACME prepaid the $70 freight. Terms were 2/10 EOM. When Century received the goods, 3 sets were defective. Century returned these sets to ACME. On April 8, Century sent a $150 partial payment. Century will pay the balance on May 6. What is Century's final payment on May 6? Assume no taxes.

List price	$(50 - 3) \times \$125 = \$5,875$
Less trade discount	$.90 \times .96 \times .98 \times \$5,875 = \$4,974.48 + \text{Freight}$
April 8 pays $150	$\dfrac{\$150}{.98} = \$153.06$

$4,974.48 - $153.06 = $4,821.42 due + $70

May 6 $4,821.42 - (.02 \times $4,821.42) = $96.43

$$\begin{array}{r} \$4,821.42 - \$96.43 = \$4,724.99 \\ +\ \ \ 70.00 \\ \hline \$4,794.99 \end{array}$$

CHAPTER 8 – Markups and Markdowns: Perishables and Breakeven Analysis

End–of–Chapter Problems

Drill Problems:

8-1.   Assume markups in Problems 8-1 to 8-5 are based on cost. Find the dollar markup and selling price for the following problems. Round answers to the nearest cent.

Item	Cost	Markup percent	Dollar markup	Selling price
HP Paulson Laptop	$700	30%	$210	$910

$S = C + M$

$S = \$700 + .30(\$700)$ Check $S = \text{Cost} \times (1 + \text{Percent markup on cost})$

$S = \$700 + \$210$

$S = \$910$ $\$910 = \$700 \times 1.30$

8-3.   Solve the cost (round to the nearest cent):

Selling price of office furniture at Staples, $6,000 $\$6,000 = C + .40C$

Percent markup on cost, 40% $\dfrac{\$6,000}{1.40} = \dfrac{1.40C}{1.40}$

Actual cost?   Check $\dfrac{\$6,000}{1.40} = \$4,285.71$ $\$4,285.71 = C$ $C = \dfrac{\text{Selling price}}{1 + \text{Percent markup on cost}}$

8-5.   Complete the following:

Cost	Selling price	Dollar markup	Percent markup on cost*
$15.10	$22.00	? $6.90	? 45.70% $\left(\dfrac{\$6.90}{\$15.10}\right)$

*Round to the nearest hundredth percent.

8-7.   Assume markups in Problems 8-7 to 8-11 are based on selling price. Find the dollar markup and cost (round answers to the nearest cent):

Item	Selling price	Markup percent	Dollar markup	Cost
Sony LCD TV	$1,000	45%	$450	$550

$\$1,000.00 = C + .45(\$1,000)$ Check

$\$1,000.00 = C + \$450$ $\$550 = \$1,000 \times .55$

$\underline{-\ 450.00} \qquad \underline{-\ 450}$ ⎡ *Note:* Markup is $C = \text{Selling price} \times (1 - \text{Percent markup on selling price})$

$\overline{\quad \$550 \quad} = C$ ⎣ on selling price, not cost.

8-9.   Solve for the selling price (round to the nearest cent):

Selling price of a complete set of pots and pans at Walmart?

40% markup on selling price

Cost, actual, $66.50

Check $\dfrac{\$66.50}{.60} = \$110.83$

$$S = \$66.50 + .40S$$
$$-\ .40S \qquad\qquad -\ .40S$$
$$\dfrac{.60S}{.60} = \dfrac{\$66.50}{.60}$$
$$S = \$110.83$$

8-11.   Complete the following:

Cost	Selling price	Dollar markup	Percent markup on selling price (round to nearest tenth percent)
$14.80	$49.00	? $34.20	? 69.8% $\left(\dfrac{\$34.20}{\$49.00}\right)$

8-15.   Complete the following:

Calculate the final selling price to the nearest cent and markdown percent to the nearest hundredth percent:

Original selling price	First markdown	Second markdown	Markup	Final markdown
$5,000	20%	10%	12%	5%

$5,000 × .80 = $4,000.00

$4,000 × .90 = $3,600.00

$3,600 × 1.12 = $4,032.00

$4,032 × .95 = $3,830.40

$\begin{array}{r}\$5,000.00\\-\ 3,830.40\\\hline\$1,169.60\end{array}$

$\dfrac{\$1,169.60}{\$5,000.00} = 23.39\%$

8-17.

Breakeven point	Fixed cost	Contribution margin	Selling price per unit	Variable cost per unit
16,250	$65,000	$4.00	$5.00	$1.00

$\dfrac{\$65,000}{\$4.00} = 16,250$

$5.00 − $1.00

Word Problems:

8-23.   Brownsville, Texas, boasts being the southernmost international seaport and the largest city in the lower Rio Grande Valley. Ben Supple, an importer in Brownsville, has just received a shipment of Peruvian opals that he is pricing for sale. He paid $150 for the shipment. If he wants a 75% markup, calculate the selling price based on selling price. Then calculate the selling price based on cost.

Selling price based on SP

$S = \$150 + .75S$

$.25S = \$150$

$S = \$600$

$S = \$150/1 − .75 = \$600$

Selling price based on cost

$S = \$150 + .75(\$150)$

$S = \$150 + \$112.50$

$S = \$262.50$

$S = \$150(1 + .75) = \$262.50$

8-24. "Approximately 57% of Americans drink coffee every day, between three and four cups on average. In fact, coffee is the second most valuable commodity in the world, after petroleum, and the largest food import in the United States," says Erin Joyce from Financial Edge Investopedia. Seattle, Washington, was the birthplace of the coffee shop era providing a cup of "joe" along with a relaxing atmosphere ripe for the gathering of friends. This atmosphere is not without cost. The latest calculations for brewing a cup of drip coffee showed cost per cup to be $.42. Purchasing a cup of drip coffee from a coffee shop costs $1.50. What is the percent markup based on cost to the nearest hundredth percent for purchasing a cup of brewed coffee?

Markup = $1.50 − .42 = $1.08

$1.08/.42 = 2.5714 = 257.14%

Check $1.50 = $.42 + 2.5714(.42)
$1.50 = $.42 + 1.08
$1.50 = $1.50

8-29. Angie's Bake Shop makes birthday chocolate chip cookies that cost $2 each. Angie expects that 10% of the cookies will crack and be discarded. Angie wants a 60% markup on cost and produces 100 cookies. What should Angie price each cookie? Round to the nearest cent.

Total cost = 100 × $2.00 = $200

Total selling price = $TC + TM$

$TS = $200 + .60($200)$

$TS = $200 + 120

$TS = 320

Selling price per cookie = $\dfrac{\$320}{90 \text{ cookies}}$ = $3.56

(100 cookies − 10%)

Additional Set of Word Problems:

8-35. At a local Bed and Bath Superstore, the manager, Jill Roe, knows her customers will pay no more than $300 for a bedspread. Jill wants a 35% markup on selling price. What is the most that Jill can pay for a bedspread?
Note: Markup is on selling price, not cost.

$300 = C + .35($300)

$300 = C + $105
− 105   − 105
$195 = C

Check

$C = \text{Selling price} \times \left(1 - \dfrac{\text{Percent markup}}{\text{on selling price}}\right)$

$195 = $300 × .65

8-39. Assume that Arley (Problem 8–38) can sell the broken cookies for $1.40 each. What should Arley price each cookie?

$\dfrac{\$435 - (30 \text{ cookies} \times \$1.40)}{170 \text{ cookies}} = \dfrac{\$435 - \$42}{170} = \$2.31$

Cumulative Review Chapters 6-8:

1. Sunset Co. marks up merchandise 40% on cost. A DVD player costs Sunset $90. What is Sunset's selling price? Round to the nearest cent. *(p. 206)*

$S = $90 + .40($90)

$S = $90 + $36

$S = $126

Check $S = \text{Cost} \times (1 + \text{Percent markup on cost})$

$126 = $90 × 1.40

3. Best Buy sells a flat-screen high-definition TV for $700. Best Buy marks up the TV 45% on cost. What is the cost and dollar markup of the TV? *(p. 206)*

$$S = C + M$$
$$\$700 = C + .45C$$
$$\frac{\$700}{1.45} = \frac{1.45C}{1.45}$$
$$\$482.76 = C$$

$$\begin{array}{r} \$700.00 \\ -482.76 \\ \hline \$217.24 \text{ markup} \end{array}$$

Check $$\text{Cost} = \frac{\text{Selling price}}{1 + \text{Percent markup on cost}}$$

$$\$482.76 = \frac{\$700}{1.45}$$

7. Zales sells diamonds for $1,100 that cost $800. What is Zales's percent markup on selling price? Round to the nearest hundredth percent. Check the selling price. *(p. 211)*

$$\frac{\$300}{\$1,100} = 27.27\%$$

Check $$\frac{\$300}{.2727} = \$1,100.11 \text{ (off due to rounding)}$$

CHAPTER 9 – Payroll

End–of–Chapter Problems

Drill Problems:

9-3.   Complete the following table (assume the overtime for each employee is a time-and-a-half rate after 40 hours:

Employee	M	T	W	Th	F	Sa	Total regular hours	Total overtime hours	Regular rate	Overtime rate	Gross earnings
. Blue	12	9	9	9	9	3	40	11	$8.00	$12.00	$452.00

$40 \times \$8 = \$320$
$11 \times \$12 = \underline{132}$
$\overline{\$452}$

9-5.   Calculate gross earnings:

Worker	Number of units produced	Rate per unit	Gross earnings
Lang	480	$3.50	$1,680 (480 × $3.50)

9-7.   Calculate the gross earnings for each apple picker based on the following differential pay scale:

| 1–1,000: $.03 each | 1,001–1,600: $.05 each | Over 1,600: $.07 each |

Apple picker	Number of apples picked	Gross earnings
Ryan	1,600	$60 = (1,000 × $.03) + (600 × $.05)

Ron Company has the following commission schedule:

Commission rate	Sales
2%	Up to $80,000
3.5%	Excess of $80,000 to $100,000
4%	More than $100,000

Calculate the gross earnings of Ron Company's two employees:

9-10.

Employee	Total sales	Gross earnings
Bill Moore	$ 70,000	$1,400 ($70,000 × .02)

9-11.   Ron Ear $155,000

$$\begin{pmatrix} \$80{,}000 \times .02 = \$1{,}600 \\ \$20{,}000 \times .035 = 700 \\ \$55{,}000 \times .04 = \underline{2{,}200} \\ \$4{,}500 \end{pmatrix}$$

Word Problems:

9-17.   Complete the following payroll register. Calculate FIT by the percentage method for this weekly period; Social Security and Medicare are the same rates as in the previous problems. No one will reach the maximum for FICA.

Employee	Marital status	Allowances claimed	Gross pay	FIT	FICA S.S.	Med.	Net pay
Jim Day	M	2	$1,400	$150.49	$86.80	$20.30	$1,142.41

S.S.: $1,400 × .062 = $86.80   Med.: $1,400 × .0145 = $20.30

FIT: $1,400.00
  − 140.38 ($70.19 × 2)
   $1,259.62 $ 30.70
  − 461.00   + 119.79 (.15 × $798.62)
   $ 798.62 $150.49

9-19.   Given the following, calculate the state (assume 5.3%) and federal unemployment taxes that the employer must pay for each of the first two quarters. The federal unemployment tax is .8% on the first $7,000.

PAYROLL SUMMARY		
	Quarter 1	Quarter 2
Bill Adams	$4,000	$ 8,000
Rich Haines	8,000	14,000
Alice Smooth	3,200	3,800

*Note only first $7,000 is taxed.
†Only first $3,000 is taxed since that puts Adams over $7,000 for the year.

Quarter 1
Adams $ 4,000
Haines   7,000*
Smooth   3,200
         $14,200
       × .053
SUTA = $752.60

Quarter 2
Adams $ 3,000†
Haines   0
Smooth   3,800
         $ 6,800
       × .053
SUTA = $360.40
FUTA = $ 54.40 ($6,800 × .008)

.008 × $14,200 = $113.60 FUTA

9-21.   Rhonda Brennan found her first job after graduating from college through the classifieds of the *Miami Herald*. She was delighted when the offer came through at $18.50 per hour. She completed her W-4 stating that she is married with a child and claims an allowance of 3. Her company will pay her biweekly for 80 hours. Calculate her take-home pay for her first check.
Gross pay: $18.50 × 80 = $1,480
Social security tax: $1,480 × .062 = $91.76
Medicare: $1,480 × .0145 = $21.46
FIT: $140.38 × 3 = $421.14; $1,480 − $421.14 = $1,058.86;
$1,058.86 − 921.00 = $137.86
$61.30 + ($137.86 × .15) = $81.98

$1,480.00 Gross
 − 91.76 Social Security
 − 21.46 Medicare
 − 81.98 FIT
$1,284.80 Net pay

9-23. Dennis Toby is a salesclerk at Northwest Department Store. Dennis receives $8 per hour plus a commission of 3% on all sales. Assume Dennis works 30 hours and has sales of $1,900. What is his gross pay?

(30 hours × $8) + ($1,900 × .03) = $240 + $57 = $297

9-27. Richard Gaziano is a manager for Health Care, Inc. Health Care deducts Social Security, Medicare, and FIT (by percentage method) from his earnings. Assume the same Social Security and Medicare rates as in Problem 9–26. Before this payroll, Richard is $1,000 below the maximum level for Social Security earnings. Richard is married, is paid weekly, and claims 2 exemptions. What is Richard's net pay for the week if he earns $1,300?

Social Security: $1,000 × .062 = $62   Medicare: $1,300 × .0145 = $18.85

$1,300 − $62 − $18.85 − $135.49 = $1,083.66

FIT: $1,300.00
    −   140.38 ($70.19 × 2)
     $1,159.62
    −   461.00 $30.70 + .15 ($698.62)
     $ 698.62 $30.70 + $104.79 = $135.49

Challenge Problem:

9-31. The Victorville, California, *Daily Press* stated that the San Bernardino County Fair hires about 150 people during fair time. Their wages range from $6.75 to $8.00. California has a state income tax of 9%. Sandy Denny earns $8.00 per hour; George Barney earns $6.75 per hour. They both worked 35 hours this week. Both are married; however, Sandy claims 2 exemptions and George claims 1 exemption. Assume a rate of 6.2% on $106,800 for Social Security and 1.45% for Medicare. (a) What is Sandy's net pay after FIT, Social Security tax, state income tax, and Medicare have been taken out? (b) What is George's net pay after the same deductions? (c) How much more is Sandy's net pay versus George's net pay? Round to the nearest cent.

a. $8.00
   × 35 hours
   $ 280 per week

FIT: $280.00
    − 140.38 ($70.19 × 2)
     $139.62
    tax = $0

S.S.: $280 × .062 = $17.36
State: $280 × .09 = $25.20
Medicare: $280 × .0145 = $4.06

$280.00 − $0 − $17.36 − $25.20 − $4.06 = $233.38

b. $ 6.75
   ×   35 hours
   $236.25 per week

FIT: $236.25
    −   70.19 ($70.19 × 1)
     $166.06
    − 154.00
     $ 12.06 × .10 = $1.21

S.S.: $236.25 × .062 = $14.65
State: $236.25 × .09 = $21.26
Medicare: $236.25 × .0145 = $3.43

$236.25 − $1.21 − $14.65 − $21.26 − $3.43 = $195.70

c. $233.38 − $195.70 = $37.68

CHAPTER 10 – Simple Interest

End–of–Chapter Problems

Drill Problems:

10-3. Calculate the simple interest and maturity value for the following problems. Round to the nearest cent as needed.

$18,000 $7\frac{1}{4}$%   9 mo. $978.75 $18,978.75

$$\$18,000 \times .0725 \times \frac{9}{12} = \$978.75$$

10-5. Complete the following, using ordinary interest: $T = \dfrac{\text{Exact no. of days}}{360}$

$585   9%   June 5   Dec. 15   193 $28.23 $613.23

    156   349

$$\$585 \times .09 \times \frac{193}{360} = \$28.23$$

10-7. Complete the following, using exact interest: $T = \dfrac{\text{Exact no. of days}}{365}$

Principal	Interest rate	Date borrowed	Date repaid	Exact time	Interest	Maturity value
$1,000	8%	Mar. 8	June 9	93	$20.38	$1,020.38
		67	160			

$$\$1,000 \times .08 \times \frac{93}{365} = \$20.38$$

10-13. Use the U.S. Rule to solve for total interest costs, balances, and final payments (use ordinary interest).

Given   Principal: $10,000, 8%, 240 days
         Partial payments: On 100th day, $4,000
                         On 180th day, $2,000

8%, 100 days, $10,000

$$I = \$10,000 \times .08 \times \frac{100}{360} = \$222.22$$

```
 $4,000.00          $10,000.00
-   222.22 ◄       -  3,777.78
 $3,777.78          $ 6,222.22  adjusted balance
```

$$\$6,222.22 \times .08 \times \frac{80}{360} = \$110.62$$

```
 $2,000.00          $6,222.22
-   110.62 ◄       - 1,889.38
 $1,889.38          $4,332.84  adjusted balance
```

$$\$4,332.84 \times .08 \times \frac{60}{360} = \$57.77$$

```
 $4,332.84
+    57.77 ◄
 $4,390.61  balance due
```

Interest paid
```
 $222.22
  110.62
+  57.77
 $390.61
```

Word Problems:

10-17. Kelly O'Brien met Jody Jansen (Problem 10–16) at Sunshine Bank and suggested she consider the loan on exact interest. Recalculate the loan for Jody under this assumption. How much would she save in interest?

$$\$2,300 \times .09 \times \frac{137}{365} = \$77.70 + \$2,300 = \$2,377.70 \qquad \text{Save } \$1.08$$

Additional Set of Word Problems:

10-25. Availability of state and federal disaster loans was the featured article in *The Enterprise Ledger* (AL) on March 14, 2007. Alabama Deputy Treasurer Anthony Leigh said the state program allows the state treasurer to place state funds in Alabama banks at 2 percent below the market interest rate. The bank then agrees to lend the funds to individuals or businesses for 2 percent below the normal charge, to help Alabama victims of disaster to secure emergency short-term loans. Laura Harden qualifies for an emergency loan. She will need $3,500 for 5 months and the local bank has an interest rate of $4\frac{3}{4}$ percent. **(a)** What would have been the maturity value of a non-emergency loan? **(b)** What will be the maturity value of the emergency loan? Round to the nearest cent.

a.
$$\begin{array}{ccc} P & R & T \end{array}$$
$$\$3,500 \times .0475 \times \frac{5}{12} = \$69.270833 = \$69.27 \text{ interest}$$

$$\begin{array}{ccc} P & I & MV \end{array}$$
$$\$3,500 + \$69.27 = \$3,569.27$$

b.
$$\begin{array}{ccc} P & R & T \end{array}$$
$$\$3,500 \times .0275 \times \frac{5}{12} = \$40.104166 = \$40.10 \text{ interest}$$

$$\begin{array}{ccc} P & I & MV \end{array}$$
$$\$3,500 + \$40.10 = \$3,540.10$$

10-29. Margie Pagano is buying a car. Her June monthly interest at $12\frac{1}{2}\%$ was $195. What was Margie's principal balance at the beginning of June? Use 360 days. Do not round the denominator before dividing.

$$\frac{\$195}{.125 \times \frac{30}{360}} = \frac{\$195}{.0104166} = \$18,720.12$$

10-31. Carol Miller went to Europe and forgot to pay her $740 mortgage payment on her New Hampshire ski house. For her 59 days overdue on her payment, the bank charged her a penalty of $15. What was the rate of interest charged by the bank? Round to the nearest hundredth percent (assume 360 days).

$$R = \frac{\$15}{\$740 \times \frac{59}{360}} = 12.37\%$$

Challenge Problem:

10-37. Janet Foster bought a computer and printer at Computerland. The printer had a $600 list price with a $100 trade discount and 2/10, n/30 terms. The computer had a $1,600 list price with a 25% trade discount but no cash discount. On the computer, Computerland offered Janet the choice of (1) paying $50 per month for 17 months with the 18th payment paying the remainder of the balance or (2) paying 8% interest for 18 months in equal payments.

a. Assume Janet could borrow the money for the printer at 8% to take advantage of the cash discount. How much would Janet save (assume 360 days)?

b. On the computer, what is the difference in the final payment between choices 1 and 2?

a. $490 \times .08 \times \dfrac{20}{360} = \$2.18$

    ($600 - $100) \times .98

    $10.00
    $\underline{-\quad 2.18}$
    $ 7.82 (savings—worth borrowing)

b. (1) $50 \times 17 = $850   Last payment $1,200 - $850 = $350

    (2) $1,200 \times .08 \times 1.5 = $144

    $1,200 + $144 = \dfrac{\$1,344}{18} = \$74.67$

    $350.00
    $\underline{-\quad 74.67}$
    $275.33

CHAPTER 11 – Promissory Notes, Simple Discount Notes and the Discount Process

End–of–Chapter Problems

Drill Problems:

11-1. Complete the following table for these simple discount notes. Use the ordinary interest method.

Amount due at maturity	Discount rate	Time	Bank discount	Proceeds
$14,000	$3\frac{3}{4}\%$	280 days	$408.33	$13,591.67

$$\$14,000 \times .0375 \times \frac{280}{360} = \$408.33 \qquad \$14,000 - \$408.33 = \$13,591.67$$

11-5. Solve for maturity value, discount period, bank discount, and proceeds (assume for Problems 11-5 and 11-6 a bank discount rate of 9%):

Face value (principal)	Rate of interest	Length of note	Maturity value	Date of note	Date note discounted	Discount period	Bank discount	Proceeds
$50,000	11%	95 days	$51,451.39	June 10	July 18	57	$733.18	$50,718.21

July 18   199 days
June 10 -161
        38 days

$$\$50,000 \times .11 \times \frac{95}{360} = \$1,451.39 + \$50,000 = \$51,451.39 \ MV$$

Discount period = $95 - 38 = 57$

Bank discount = $\$51,451.39 \times .09 \times \frac{57}{360} = \$733.18$

Proceeds = $\$51,451.39 - \$733.18 = \$50,718.21$

Word Problems:

11-9. Use ordinary interest as needed:

Bill Blank signed an $8,000 note at Citizen's Bank. Citizen's charges a $6\frac{1}{2}\%$ discount rate. If the loan is for 300 days, find (a) the proceeds and (b) the effective rate charged by the bank (to the nearest tenth percent).

a. $\$8,000 \times .065 \times \frac{300}{360} = \$433.33$

    $\$8,000 - \$433.33 = \$7,566.67$

b. $\dfrac{\$433.33}{\$7,566.67 \times \frac{300}{360}} = \dfrac{\$433.33}{\$6,305.5583} = 6.9\%$

11-11. On September 5, Sheffield Company discounted at Sunshine Bank a $9,000 (maturity value), 120-day note dated June 5. Sunshine's discount rate was 9%. What proceeds did Sheffield Company receive?

Sept. 5   248 days
June 5 -156
        92 days passed
$120 - 92 = 28$ days
        (discount period)

$$\$9,000 \times .09 \times \frac{28}{360} = \$63 \qquad \$9,000 - \$63 = \$8,937$$

11-17. Hafers, an electrical supply company, sold $4,800 of equipment to Jim Coates Wiring, Inc. Coates signed a promissory note May 12 with 4.5% interest. The due date was August 10. Short of funds, Hafers contacted Charter One Bank on July 20; the bank agreed to take over the note at a 6.2% discount. What proceeds will Hafers receive?

Aug. 10	222 days	$4,800 \times .045 \times \dfrac{90}{360} = \$54.00$
May 12	−132 days	
	90 length of loan	$4,800 + \$54.00 = \$4,854.00$ *MV*

July 20	201 days	$4,854.00 \times .062 \times \dfrac{21}{360} = \$17.56$ Bank discount
May 12	−132 days	
	69 days passed	$4,854.00
$90 - 69 = 21$ days		− 17.56
	(discount period)	$4,836.44 proceeds

Challenge Problem:

11-19. Tina Mier must pay a $2,000 furniture bill. A finance company will loan Tina $2,000 for 8 months at a 9% discount rate. The finance company told Tina that if she wants to receive exactly $2,000, she must borrow more than $2,000. The finance company gave Tina the following formula:

$$\text{What to ask for} = \frac{\text{Amount in cash to be received}}{1 - (\text{Discount} \times \text{Time of loan})}$$

Calculate Tina's loan request and the effective rate of interest to nearest hundredth percent.

$$\frac{\$2,000}{1 - \left(.09 \times \dfrac{8}{12}\right)} = \frac{\$2,000}{1 - .06} = \frac{\$2,000}{.94} = \$2,127.66$$

Check

$$\$2,127.66 \times .09 \times \frac{8}{12} = \$127.66$$

$$\frac{\$127.66}{\$2,000 \times \dfrac{8}{12}} = 9.57\%$$

CHAPTER 12 – Compound Interest and Present Value

End–of–Chapter Problems

Drill Problems:

12-1. Complete the following without using Table 12.1 (round to the nearest cent for each calculation) and then check by Table 12.1 (check will be off due to rounding):

Principal	Time (years)	Rate of compound interest	Compounded	Periods	Rate	Total amount	Total interest
$1,600	2	6%	Semiannually	4	3%	$1,800.81	$200.81

2 years × 2 = 4 periods $\frac{6\%}{2} = 3\%$

$1,600.00	$1,648.00	$1,697.44	$1,748.36	
× 1.03	× 1.03	× 1.03	× 1.03	Check $1,600 × 1.1255 = $1,800.80
$1,648.00	$1,697.44	$1,748.36	$1,800.31	

12-3. Complete the following using compound future value Table 12.1:

Time	Principal	Rate	Compounded	Amount	Interest
6 months	$10,000	8%	Quarterly	$10,404.00	$404.00

$\frac{6}{12} × 4 = 2$ periods $\frac{8\%}{4} = 2\%$ $10,000 × 1.0404 = $

$$\begin{array}{r} \$10,404 \\ - 10,000 \\ \hline \$ \quad 404 \end{array}$$

12-5. Calculate the effective rate (APY) of interest for 1 year:

Principal: $15,500 $15,500 × 1.1255 = $17,445.25 $\frac{\$1,945.25}{\$15,500} = .1255 = 12.55\%$
Interest rate: 12%   − 15,500.00
Compounded quarterly $ 1,945.25
Effective rate (APY): 12.55%   4 periods, $\frac{12\%}{4} = 3\%$

12-7. Complete the following using present value of Table 12.3 or *Business Math Handbook* Table:

Amount desired at end of period	Length of time	Rate	Compounded	On PV Table 12.3 Period used	On PV Table 12.3 Rate used	PV factor used	PV of amount desired at end of period
$6,000	8 years	3%	Semiannually	16	$1\frac{1}{2}\%$	.7880	$4,728.00
			$6,000 × .7880 = $4,728				

Word Problems:

12-13. Lynn Ally, owner of a local Subway shop, loaned $40,000 to Pete Hall to help him open a Subway franchise. Pete plans to repay Lynn at the end of 8 years with 6% interest compounded semiannually. How much will Lynn receive at the end of 8 years?

8 years × 2 = 16 periods $\frac{6\%}{2} = 3\%$ $40,000 × 1.6047 = $64,188

12-17. Lee Wills loaned Audrey Chin $16,000 to open Snip Its Hair Salon. After 6 years, Audrey will repay Lee with 8% interest compounded quarterly. How much will Lee receive at the end of 6 years?

6 years $\times$ 4 = 24 periods $\qquad \dfrac{8\%}{4} = 2\%$ $\qquad$ $16,000 \times 1.6084 = \$25,734.40$

12-21. Security National Bank is quoting 1-year certificates of deposit with an interest rate of 5% compounded semiannually. Joe Saver purchased a $5,000 CD. What is the CD's effective rate (APY) to the nearest hundredth percent? Use tables in the *Business Math Handbook*.

1 year $\times$ 2 = 2 periods $\qquad \dfrac{5\%}{2} = 2\tfrac{1}{2}\%$ $\qquad$ Effective rate (APY) $= \dfrac{\$253}{\$5,000} = 5.06\%$

$\begin{aligned} &\$5,000 \\ \times\, &1.0506 \\ \hline &\$5,253 \\ -\, &5,000 \\ \hline \$\,&253 \text{ interest} \end{aligned}$

12-25. Pete Air wants to buy a used Jeep in 5 years. He estimates the Jeep will cost $15,000. Assume Pete invests $10,000 now at 12% interest compounded semiannually. Will Pete have enough money to buy his Jeep at the end of 5 years?

Compounding		or	Present value	
5 years $\times$ 2 = 10 periods	$\dfrac{12\%}{2} = 6\%$		10 periods	$15,000 \times .5584 = \$8,376$
$10,000 \times 1.7908 = \$17,908$	Yes.		6%	Yes.

12-27. Paul Havlik promised his grandson Jamie that he would give him $6,000 8 years from today for graduating from high school. Assume money is worth 6% interest compounded semiannually. What is the present value of this $6,000?

8 years $\times$ 2 = 16 periods $\qquad \dfrac{6\%}{2} = 3\%$ $\qquad$ $6,000 \times .6232 = \$3,739.20$

12-31. Linda Roy received a $200,000 inheritance after taxes from her parents. She invested it at 4% interest compounded quarterly for 3 years. A year later, she sold one of her rental properties for $210,000 and invested that money at 3% compounded semi-annually for 2 years. Both of the investments have matured. She is hoping to have at least $500,000 in 7 years compounded annually at 2% interest so she can move to Hawaii. Will she meet her goal?

Inheritance investment:

3 years $\times$ 4 = 12
4% $\div$ 4 = 1%

$200,000 \times 1.1268 = \$225,360$

Rental property:

2 years $\times$ 2 = 4

$\dfrac{3\%}{2} = 1.5\%$

$210,000 \times 1.0614 = \$222,894$

Matured investment = $225,360 + \$222,894 = \$448,254$

Final amount:

7 years $\times$ 1 = 7

$\dfrac{2\%}{1} = 2\%$

$448,254 \times 1.1487 = \$514,909.36$ Linda has surpassed her goal

CHAPTER 13 – Annuities and Sinking Funds

End–of–Chapter Problems

Drill Problems:

13-1. Complete the ordinary annuities for the following using tables in the *Business Math Handbook*:

Amount of payment	Payment payable	Years	Interest rate	Value of annuity
$15,000	Quarterly	8	6% $1\frac{1}{2}\%$	$610,321.50
	32	40.6881		($15,000 × 40.6881)

13-3. Redo Problem 13-1 as an annuity due:

$15,000, 33 periods, $1\frac{1}{2}\%$ = $15,000 × 42.2984 =

$$\begin{array}{r} \$634,476 \\ -\ 15,000 \\ \hline \$619,476 \end{array}$$

13-4. Calculate the value of the following annuity due without a table. Check your results by Table 13.1 or the Business Math Handbook (they will be slight off due to rounding):

Amount of payment	Payment payable	Years	Interest rate
$2,000	Annually	3	6%

$$\begin{array}{l} \$2,000.00 \\ +\ \ \ 120.00 \\ \hline \$2,120.00 \\ +\ 2,000.00 \\ \hline \$4,120.00 \\ +\ \ \ 247.20 \\ \hline \$4,367.20 \end{array} \qquad \begin{array}{l} \$4,367.20 \\ +\ 2,000.00 \\ \hline \$6,367.20 \\ +\ \ \ 382.03 \\ \hline \$6,749.23 \end{array}$$

Check   4 periods, 6%

$2,000 × 4.3746 =

$$\begin{array}{r} \$8,749.20 \\ -\ 2,000.00 \\ \hline \$6,749.20 \end{array}$$

13-5. Complete the following using Table 13.2 or the Business Math Handbook for the present value of an ordinary annuity:

Amount of annuity expected	Payment	Time	Interest rate	Present value (amount needed now to invest to receive annuity)
$900	Annually	4 years	6%	$3,118.59 ($900 × 3.4651) (4 periods, 6%)

13-7.   Check Problem 13-5 without the use of Table 13.2:

($3,118.59 × .06)	$3,118.59	$2,405.71	$1,650.05	$849.05	
	+ 187.12	+ 144.34	+ 99.00	+ 50.94*	
	$3,305.71	$2,550.05	$1,749.05	$899.99	
	− 900.00	− 900.00	− 900.00	− 900.00	
	$2,405.71	$1,650.05	$ 849.05	$ .00	*Off 1 cent due to rounding.

13-8.   Using the sinking fund Table 13.3 or the *Business Math Handbook*, complete the following:

Required amount	Frequency of payment	Length of time	Interest rate	Payment amount end of each period
$25,000	Quarterly	6 years	8%	$822.50 (24 periods, 2% = .0329) $25,000 × .0329 = $822.50

13-9.

$15,000	Annually	8 years	8%	$1,410 (8 periods, 8% = .0940) $15,000 × .0940 = $1,410

Word Problems:

13-3.   "The most powerful force in the universe is compound interest," according to an article in the *Morningstar Column* dated February 13, 2007. Patricia Wiseman is 30 years old and she invests $2,000 in an annuity, earning 5% compound annual return at the beginning of each period, for 18 years. What is the cash value of this annuity due at the end of 18 years?
18 periods + 1 = 19, 5%

30.5389
× $ 2,000
$61,077.80
− 2,000.00
$59,077.80

13-15.   The average American has $99 lying about. Stick $99 in an ordinary annuity account each year for 10 years at 5% interest and watch it grow. What is the cash value of this annuity at the end of year 10? Round to the nearest dollar.
10 periods, 5% 12.5779 (Table 13.1)
$99 × 12.5779 = $1,245.2121 = $1,245

13-21.   At the beginning of each period for 10 years, Merl Agnes invests $500 semiannually at 6%. What is the cash value of this annuity due at the end of year 10?
20 periods + 1 = 21, 3% $500 × 28.6765 = $14,338.25
                                            − 500.00
                                            $13,838.25

13-23. On Joe Martin's graduation from college, Joe's uncle promised him a gift of $12,000 in cash or $900 every quarter for the next 4 years after graduation. If money could be invested at 8% compounded quarterly, which offer is better for Joe?

16 periods, $\frac{8\%}{4} = 2\%$ $900 \times 13.5777 = \$12,219.93$ or $900 \times 18.6392 =$ $\$16,775.28$

(Table 13.2)   (Table 13.1) $\times$ .7284 (Table 12.3)

$\$12,219.11$

Choose the annuity.   2%   16 periods

13-25. A local Dunkin' Donuts franchise must buy a new piece of equipment in 5 years that will cost $88,000. The company is setting up a sinking fund to finance the purchase. What will the quarterly deposit be if the fund earns 8% interest?
20 periods, 2% (Table 13.3)

$.0412 \times \$88,000 = \$3,625.60$ quarterly payment

13-31. Ajax Corporation has hired Brad O'Brien as its new president. Terms included the company's agreeing to pay retirement benefits of $18,000 at the end of each semiannual period for 10 years. This will begin in 3,285 days. If the money can be invested at 8% compounded semiannually, what must the company deposit today to fulfill its obligation to Brad?

10 years $\times$ 2 = 20 periods $\frac{8\%}{2} = 4\%$

$\$18,000 \times 13.5903 = \$244,625.40$ (Table 13.2)

$\frac{3,285 \text{ days}}{365 \text{ days per year}} = 9 \text{ years}$ 9 years $\times$ 2 = 18 periods $\frac{8\%}{2} = 4\%$

$\$244,625.40 \times .4936 = \$120,747.09$ (Table 12.3)

Check $\$120,747.09 \times 2.0258 = \$244,609.45$ (off due to rounding)   (Table 12.1)

Cumulative Review Chapters 10-13:

1. Lin Lowe plans to deposit $1,800 at the end of every 6 months for the next 15 years at 8% interest compounded semiannually. What is the value of Lin's annuity at the end of 15 years? *(p. 317)*
    30 periods, 4% $1,800 \times 56.0849 = \$100,952.82$
    (Table 13.1)

3. Sanka Blunck wants to receive $8,000 each year for 20 years. How much must Sanka invest today at 4% interest compounded annually? *(p. 324)*
    20 periods, 4% (Table 13.2) $\$8,000 \times 13.5903 = \$108,722.40$

5. Lance Industries borrowed $130,000. The company plans to set up a sinking fund that will repay the loan at the end of 18 years. Assume a 6% interest rate compounded semiannually. What amount must Lance Industries pay into the fund each period? Check your answer by Table 13.1 *(p. 325)*
    36 periods, 3% $\$130,000 \times .0158 = \$2,054$ **Check** $\$2,054 \times 63.2759 = \$129,968.69^*$

    *Off due to table rounding.

7. Twice a year for 15 years, Warren Ford invested $1,700 compounded semiannually at 6% interest. What is the value of this annuity due? *(p. 319)*
    31 periods, 3% (Table 13.1) $1,700 \times 50.0027 =$ $\$85,004.59$
    $-$ 1,700.00
    $\$83,304.59$

CHAPTER 14 – Installment Buying, Rule of 78 and Revolving Charge Credit Cards

End–of–Chapter Problems

Drill Problems:

14-1.   Complete the following table.

Purchase price of product	Down payment	Amount financed	Number of monthly payments	Amount of monthly payments	Total of monthly payments	Total finance charge
Acura MDX $35,000	− $10,000	= $25,000	72 ×	$380 =	$27,360	$2,360 ($27,360 − $25,000)

14-3.   Calculate **(a)** the amount financed, **(b)** the total finance charge, and **(c)** APR by table lookup:

Purchase price of a used car	Down payment	Number of monthly payments	Amount financed	Total of monthly payments	Total finance charge	APR
$5,673	$1,223	48	$4,450	$5,729.76	$1,279.76	12.75%–13%

$$\begin{array}{r} \$5,673 \\ -\ 1,223 \\ \hline \$4,450 \end{array} \qquad \begin{array}{r} \$5,729.76 \\ -\ 4,450.00 \\ \hline \$1,279.76 \end{array}$$

$\dfrac{\$1,279.76}{\$4,450.00} \times \$100 = \$28.76$ is between 12.75% and 13% at 48 months

14-5.   Calculate the monthly payment for Problems 14-3 by table lookup and formula. (Answers will not be exact due to rounding of percents in table lookup).

(14–3) (Use 13% for table lookup.)

Table: $\begin{array}{r} \$5,673 \\ -\ 1,223 \\ \hline \$4,450 \end{array} \div \$1,000 = \begin{array}{r} 4.45 \\ \times\ 26.83 \text{ (13\%, 48 months)} \\ \hline \$119.39 \end{array}$

Formula: $\dfrac{\$1,279.76 + \$4,450}{48} = \$119.37$

14-7.   Calculate the finance charge rebate and payoff:

Loan	Months of loan	End-of-month loan is repaid	Monthly payment	Finance charge rebate	Final payoff
$7,000	36	10	$210	$295.14	$5,164.86

Step 1.
Total payments
$\begin{array}{rr} 36 \times \$210 = & \$7,560 \\ 10 \times \$210 = & -\ 2,100 \\ \hline \text{Balance outstanding} & \$5,460 \end{array}$

Step 2.
$\begin{array}{lr} \text{Total of all payments } 36 \times \$210 & \$7,560 \\ \text{Amount financed} & -\ 7,000 \\ \hline \text{Total finance charge} & \$\ 560 \end{array}$

14-7. **Step 3.** $36 - 10 = 26$

Step 4. By Table 14.3 $\dfrac{351 \rightarrow}{666 \rightarrow}$ 26 months to go / 36 months total loan

Step 5. $\dfrac{351}{666} \times \$560 = \$295.14$ finance charge rebate

(Step 4) (Step 2)

Step 6. $\$5,460 - \$295.14 = \$5,164.86$ (payoff)

(Step 1)　(Step 5)

14-9. Calculate the average daily balance and finance charge

30-day billing cycle				No. of days of current balance	Current balance	Extension
9/16	Billing date	Previous balance	$2,000	3	$2,000	$ 6,000
9/19	Payment		$ 60	11	1,940	21,340
9/30	Charge: Home Depot		1,500	3	3,440	10,320
10/3	Payment		60	4	3,380	13,520
10/7	Cash advance		70	9	3,450	31,050
Finance charge is $1\frac{1}{2}$% on average daily balance						

$\dfrac{\$82,230}{30} =$ $\$2,741$ average daily balance

$\times \quad .015$

$\overline{\$41.12}$ finance charge

Word Problems:

14-11. To help consumers in this tough economic climate, Pikes Peak Harley-Davidson offered to finance a new motorcycle for qualifying customers at 15% down, 7.5% interest for 48 months during July 2009. Rich Martinez was interested in calculating what his monthly payment would be if he bought a $29,386 bike. Use the loan amortization table to calculate his monthly payment to the nearest cent.

$\$29,386 \times 0.15 = \$4,407.90$

$\$29,386 - \$4,407.90 = \$24,978.10$

$\$24,978.10 \div \$1,000 = \$24.98 \times 24.18 = \$604.07$

14-13. From this partial advertisement calculate:

$95.10 per month
#43892 Used car. Cash price $4,100. Down payment $50. For 60 months.

a. Amount financed.
b. Finance charge.
c. Deferred payment price.
d. APR by Table 14.1.
e. Check monthly payment (by formula).

a. Amount financed $= \$4,100 - \$50 = \$4,050$

b. Finance charge $= \$5,706 \ (\$95.10 \times 60) - \$4,050 = \$1,656$

c. Deferred payment price $= \$5,706 \ (\$95.10 \times 60) + \$50 = \$5,756$

d. $\dfrac{\$1,656}{\$4,050} \times \$100 = \$40.89$ (Table 14.1, between 14.25% and 14.50%)

e. $\dfrac{\$1,656 + \$4,050}{60} = \$95.10$

14-17. First America Bank's monthly payment charge on a 48-month $20,000 loan is $488.26. The U.S. Bank's monthly payment fee is $497.70 for the same loan amount. What would be the APR for an auto loan for each of these banks? (Use the *Business Math Handbook*.)

First America Bank

$488.26 \times 48 = \quad \$23,436.48$
$$\underline{-\ 20,000.00}$$
$$\$\ 3,436.48 \text{ finance charge}$$

$\dfrac{\$3,436.48}{\$20,000} \times \$100 = \$17.1824$

$= \text{Between } 8.00\% \text{ and } 8.25\%$

U.S. Bank

$497.70 \times 48 = \quad \$23,889.60$
$$\underline{-\ 20,000.00}$$
$$\$\ 3,889.60 \text{ finance charge}$$

$\dfrac{\$3,889.60}{\$20,000} \times \$100 = \$19.45$

$= \text{Between } 8.75\% \text{ and } 9\%$

Challenge Problem:

14-21. You have a $1,100 balance on your 15% credit card. You have lost your job and been unemployed for 6 months. You have been unable to make any payments on your balance. However, you received a tax refund and want to pay off the credit card. How much will you owe on the credit card, and how much interest will have accrued? What will be the effective rate of interest after the 6 months (to the nearest hundredth percent)?

Interest

1 month: $\$1,100.00 \times .15 \times \frac{1}{12} = \$13.75 = \$1,113.75$

2 months: $\$1,113.75 \times .15 \times \frac{1}{12} = \$13.92 = \$1,127.67$

3 months: $\$1,127.67 \times .15 \times \frac{1}{12} = \$14.10 = \$1,141.77$

4 months: $\$1,141.77 \times .15 \times \frac{1}{12} = \$14.27 = \$1,156.04$

5 months: $\$1,156.04 \times .15 \times \frac{1}{12} = \$14.45 = \$1,170.49$

6 months: $\$1,170.49 \times .15 \times \frac{1}{12} = \$14.63 = \$1,185.12$

$\dfrac{\$85.12 \text{ interest}}{\$1,100 \times \frac{6}{12}} = \dfrac{\$85.12}{\$550} = 15.48\%$

CHAPTER 15 – The Cost of Home Ownership

End–of–Chapter Problems

Drill Problems:

15-1.   Complete the following amortization chart by using Table 15.1:

Selling price of home	Down payment	Principal (loan)	Rate of interest	Years	Payment per $1,000	Monthly mortgage payment
$120,000	$10,000	$110,000	5%	25	$5.85	$643.50 (110 × $5.85)

15-7.   Complete the following:

Selling price	Down payment	Amount mortgage	Rate	Years	Monthly payment	First Payment Broken Down Into—		Balance at end of month
						Interest	Principal	
$199,000	$40,000	$159,000	12½%	35	$1,679.04	$1,656.25	$22.79	$158,977.21

$$159 \times \$10.56 = \$1,679.04; \$159,000 \times .125 \times \frac{1}{12} = \$1,656.25 \qquad (\$159,000 - \$22.79)$$

Word Problems:

15-9.   In the summer of 2009, a man woke to an early morning fire causing $150,000 damage to his home in Avon, Ohio, the *Cleveland Plain Dealer* noted. The man decided to purchase a second home to live in during his home's reconstruction. When the repairs were done, he would turn one of the homes into a rental property. He purchased his second home for $215,000 at 5% for 30 years and put down 20% to avoid paying private mortgage insurance. Calculate his monthly payment.
$215,000 × 0.2 = $43,000

$215,000 − $43,000 = $172,000

$172,000 ÷ $1,000 = 172 × $5.37 = $923.64

15-11.   Joe Levi bought a home in Arlington, Texas, for $140,000. He put down 20% and obtained a mortgage for 30 years at 5½%. What is Joe's monthly payment? What is the total interest cost of the loan?
$140,000 − $28,000 = $112,000/$1,000 = 112 × $5.68 = $636.16 × 360 = $229,017.60 − $112,000 = $117,017.60 total interest

15-13. Mike Jones bought a new split-level home for $150,000 with 20% down. He decided to use Victory Bank for his mortgage. They were offering $13\frac{3}{4}\%$ for 25-year mortgages. Provide Mike with an amortization schedule for the first three periods.

Payment number	Portion to— Interest	Portion to— Principal	Balance of loan outstanding	Monthly payment is:
1	$1,375.00	$47.00 ($1,422 − $1,375)	$119,953.00 ($120,000 − $47.00)	$\dfrac{\$120,000}{\$1,000} = 120 \times \$11.85 = \$1,422$
2	$1,374.46	$47.54 ($1,422.00 − $1,374.46)	$119,905.46 ($119,953.00 − $47.54)	$\$120,000 \times .1375 \times \dfrac{1}{12} = \$1,375.00$
3	$1,373.92	$48.08	$119,857.38	$\$119,953.00 \times .1375 \times \dfrac{1}{12} = \$1,374.46$
				$\$119,905.46 \times .1375 \times \dfrac{1}{12} = \$1,373.92$

Challenge Problem:

15-17. Tony Saulino recently refinanced his $265,000 home from a 7.5%, 30-year mortgage to a 5%, 15-year mortgage. Calculate the monthly payment for both mortgages. Then calculate an estimate of how much interest he is saving with the 15-year mortgage.
$265,000 \div \$1,000 = 265$

30 year: $265 \times 7.00 = \$1,855 \times 360 = \$667,800$

15 year: $265 \times 7.91 = \$2,096.15 \times 180 = \$377,307$

Total interest saved: $667,800 − $377,307 = $290,493

CHAPTER 16 – How to Read, Analyze and Interpret Financial Reports

End–of–Chapter Problems

Drill Problems:

16-1. As the accountant for a local Petco store, prepare a December 31, 2012, balance sheet like that for The Card Shop (LU 16–1) from the following: cash, $30,000; accounts payable, $18,000; merchandise inventory, $14,000; Vic Sullivan, capital, $46,000; and equipment, $20,000.

PETCO
Balance Sheet
December 31, 2012

Assets		Liabilities	
Cash	$30,000	Accounts payable	$18,000
Merchandise Inventory	14,000	**Owner's Equity**	
Equipment	20,000	Vic Sullivan, capital	46,000
Total assets	$64,000	Total liabilities and owner's equity	$64,000

16-7. Complete the comparative income statement and balance sheet for Logic Company (round percents to the nearest hundredth):

LOGIC COMPANY
Comparative Income Statement
For Years Ended December 31, 2012 and 2013

	2013	2012	INCREASE (DECREASE) Amount	INCREASE (DECREASE) Percent
Gross sales	$19,000	$15,000	$4,000	26.67
Sales returns and allowances	1,000	100	900	900.00
Net sales	$18,000	$14,900	$3,100	+ 20.81
Cost of merchandise (goods) sold	12,000	9,000	3,000	+ 33.33
Gross profit	$ 6,000	$ 5,900	$ 100	+ 1.69
Operating expenses:				
Depreciation	$ 700	$ 600	$ 100	+ 16.67
Selling and administrative	2,200	2,000	200	+ 10.00
Research	550	500	50	+ 10.00
Miscellaneous	360	300	60	+ 20.00
Total operating expenses	$ 3,810	$ 3,400	$ 410	+ 12.06
Income before interest and taxes	$ 2,190	$ 2,500	$ (310)	− 12.40
Interest expense	560	500	60	+ 12.00
Income before taxes	$ 1,630	$ 2,000	$ (370)	− 18.50
Provision for taxes	640	800	(160)	− 20.00
Net income	$ 990	$ 1,200	$ (210)	− 17.50

$3,100
$14,900

16-7.

LOGIC COMPANY Comparative Balance Sheet December 31, 2012 and 2013				
	2013		**2012**	
	Amount	Percent	Amount	Percent
Assets				
Current assets:				
Cash	$12,000	13.48	$ 9,000	13.74
Accounts receivable	16,500	18.54	12,500	19.08
Merchandise inventory	8,500	9.55	14,000	21.37
Prepaid expenses	24,000	26.97	10,000	15.27
Total current assets	$61,000	68.54	$45,500	69.47*
Plant and equipment:				
Building (net)	$14,500	16.29	$11,000	16.79
Land	13,500	15.17	9,000	13.74
Total plant and equipment	$28,000	31.46	$20,000	30.53
Total assets	$89,000	100.00	$65,500	100.00
Liabilities				
Current liabilities:				
Accounts payable	$13,000	14.61	$ 7,000	10.69
Salaries payable	7,000	7.87	5,000	7.63
Total current liabilities	$20,000	22.47*	$12,000	18.32
Long-term liabilities:				
Mortgage note payable	22,000	24.72	20,500	31.30
Total liabilities	$42,000	47.19	$32,500	49.62
Stockholders' Equity				
Common stock	$21,000	23.60	$21,000	32.06
Retained earnings	26,000	29.21	12,000	18.32
Total stockholders' equity	$47,000	52.81	$33,000	50.38
Total liabilities and stockholders' equity	$89,000	100.00	$65,500	100.00

$\dfrac{\$9,000}{\$65,500}$

*Due to rounding.

16-9. From Problem 16-7, your supervisor has requested that you calculate the following ratios (round to the nearest hundredth):

	2013	2012
Acid test.	1.43	1.79

$\dfrac{CA - Inv - \text{Prepaid expenses}}{CL}$ $\dfrac{\$61,000 - \$8,500 - \$24,000}{\$20,000} = 1.43$ $\dfrac{\$45,500 - \$14,000 - \$10,000}{\$12,000} = 1.79$

16-13. Net income (after tax) to the net sales.   .06   .08

$\dfrac{NI}{\text{Net sales}}$ $\dfrac{\$990}{\$18,000} = .055 = .06$ $\dfrac{\$1,200}{\$14,900} = .0805 = .08$

Word Problems:

16-15. The March 2009 edition of *Kiplinger's Personal Finance* reported on what to do if you were victimized by Bernard Madoff's alleged Ponzi scheme. Recommendations include: ensure there is a third-party custodian, beware of group connections, and investigate who audits your advisor. Holocaust survivor Elie Wiesel's Foundation for Humanity lost $15.2 million of his charity's (stockholders equity) money. If he had been promised a 10% return on equity, what was the anticipated return?

Return on equity: $X \div \$15.2 = 10\%$

$X = 0.10(\$15.2)$
$X = \$1.52$ million

16-17. Find the following ratios for Motorola Credit Corporation's annual report: (a) total debt to total assets, (b) return on equity, (c) asset turnover (to nearest cent), and (d) profit margin on net sales. Round to the nearest hundredth percent.

	(dollars in millions)
Net revenue (sales)	$ 265
Net earnings	147
Total assets	2,015
Total liabilities	1,768
Total stockholders' equity	427

a. $\dfrac{\text{Total liabilities}}{\text{Total assets}}$ $\dfrac{\$1,768}{\$2,015} = 87.74\%$

b. $\dfrac{\text{Net income}}{\text{Stockholders' equity}}$ $\dfrac{\$147}{\$427} = 34.43\%$

c. $\dfrac{\text{Net sales}}{\text{Total assets}}$ $\dfrac{\$265}{\$2,015} = .13$

d. $\dfrac{\text{Net income}}{\text{Net sales}}$ $\dfrac{\$147}{\$265} = 55.47\%$

Challenge Problem:

16-20. PepsiCo reported 2008 revenue of $43,251 million, net income of $5,142 million, total assets of $35,994 million, and EPS of $3.21. Common shareholders had $12,203 million in equity. In 2007 they reported revenue of $39,474 million, net income of $5,658 million, total assets of $34,628 million, and EPS of $3.41. Common shareholders had $17,325 million in equity. (a) What is the return on equity for each year? Round to the nearest hundredth percent. (b) What is the profit margin on net sales for each year? Round to the nearest hundredth percent as needed. (c) What is the asset turnover for each year? Round to the nearest hundredth percent. Analyze each ratio and mark which year had a better outcome.

2008	**2007**
a. $5,142 \div \$12,203 = 42.14\%$ Best	$5,658 \div \$17,325 = 32.66\%$
b. $5,142 \div \$43,251 = 11.89\%$ Best	$5,658 \div \$39,474 = 14.33\%$
c. $43,251 \div \$35,994 = 1.20$ Best	$39,474 \div 34,628 = 1.14$

CHAPTER 17 – Depreciation

End–of–Chapter Problems

Drill Problems:

From the following facts, complete a depreciation schedule using the straight-line method:

Given Cost of Toyota Hybrid Highlander $30,000
           Residual value $ 6,000
           Estimated life   8 years

	End of year	Cost of Highlander	Depreciation expense for year	Accumulated depreciation at end of year	Book value at end of year	
17-1.	1	$30,000	$3,000	$3,000	$27,000 ($30,000 − $3,000)	$\frac{\$30,000 - \$6,000}{8 \text{ years}} = \$3,000$
17-7.	7	$30,000	$3,000	$21,000	$9,000	

Given Volvo truck $25,000   Prepare a depreciation using the declining-balance
           Residual value $ 5,000   (twice the straight-line rate)
           Estimated life   5 years

	End of year	Cost of truck	Accumulated depreciation at beginning of year	Book value at beginning of year	Depreciation expense for year	Accumulated depreciation at end of year	Book value at end of year
17-9.	1	$25,000	–0–	$25,000	$10,000 ($25,000 × .40)	$10,000	$15,000 ($25,000 − $10,000)
17-10.	2	$25,000	$10,000	$15,000	$6,000 ($15,000 × .40)	$16,000	$9,000 ($25,000 − $16,000)
17-11.	3	$25,000	$16,000	$9,000	$3,600 ($9,000 × .40)	$19,600	$5,400 ($25,000 − $19,600)
17-12.	4	$25,000	$19,600	$5,400	$400* ($5,400 − $5,000)	$20,000	$5,000

*Cannot be depreciated below book value.

Word Problem:

17-25. Perry Wiseman of Truckers Accounting Service in Omaha, Nebraska, likes to use the straight-line method and take a little bit extra the first year, so there are three good years of depreciation. The cost of his truck was $108,000, with a useful life of 3 years and a residual value of $35,000. What would be the book value of the truck after the first year? Round your answers to the nearest dollar.

$$\frac{\$108,000 - \$35,000}{3} = \$24,333.333 = \$24,333 \text{ depreciation each year}$$

$108,000 - $24,333 = $83,667 book value after first year

Challenge Problem:

17-27. Assume a piece of equipment was purchased July 26, 2012, at a cost of $72,000. The estimated residual value is $5,400 with a useful life of 5 years. Assume a production life of 60,000 units. Compute the depreciation for years 2012 and 2013 using (a) straight-line and (b) units-of-production (in 2012, 5,000 units produced and in 2013, 18,000 units produced).

a. $\dfrac{\$72,000 - \$5,400}{5 \text{ years}} = \$13,320$

b. $\dfrac{\$72,000 - \$5,400}{60,000} = \$1.11$

2012: $13,320 \times \dfrac{5}{12} = \$5,550^{(5/12 \text{ Aug. to Dec. 31})}$

2012: $5,000 \times \$1.11 = \$5,550$

2013: $13,320

2013: $18,000 \times \$1.11 = \$19,980$

48

CHAPTER 18 – Inventory and Overhead

End–of–Chapter Problems

Drill Problems:

18-1. Using the specific identification method, calculate (a) the ending inventory and (b) the cost of goods sold given the following:

Date	Units purchased	Cost per iPod		Ending inventory
June 1	12 Blackberrys	$ 99	$ 1,188	7 Blackberrys from June 1
October 1	30 Blackberrys	109	3,270	9 Blackberrys from Oct. 1
December 1	37 Blackberrys	125	4,625	10 Blackberrys from Dec. 1

June 1	4 Blackberrys × $ 99 = $ 396	$9,083
October 1	7 Blackberrys × $109 = 763	
December 1	10 Blackberrys × $125 = 1,250	$9,083 cost of goods available for sale
	$2,409	− 2,409 (a) cost of ending inventory
		$6,674 (b) cost of goods sold

From the following, **(a)** calculate the cost of ending inventory (round the average unit cost to the nearest cent) and **(b)** cost of goods sold using the weighted-average method, FIFO and LIFO (ending inventory shows 61 units).

	Number purchased	Cost per unit	Total
January 1 inventory	40	$4	$160
April 1	60	7	420
June 1	50	8	400
November 1	55	9	495
	205		$1,475

18-3. FIFO:

$$55 \times \$9 = \$495$$
$$6 \times 8 = + \underline{48}$$

a. Cost of ending inventory	$543	FIFO—old sold first.
Cost of goods available for sale	$1,475	
Ending inventory	− 543	
b. Cost of goods sold	$ 932	

From the following calculate the cost of ending inventory and cost of goods sold for LIFO (18-13), FIFO (18-14), and the weighted-average (18-15) methods (make sure to first find total cost to complete the table); ending inventory is 49 units:

Beginning inventory and purchases	Units	Unit cost	Total dollar cost
Beginning inventory, January 1	5	$2.00	$ 10.00
April 10	10	2.50	25.00
May 15	12	3.00	36.00
July 22	15	3.25	48.75
August 19	18	4.00	72.00
September 30	20	4.20	84.00
November 10	32	4.40	140.80
December 15	16	4.80	76.80
	128		$493.35

18-13. LIFO:

Cost of ending inventory

$$5 \text{ at } \$2.00 = \$ \ 10.00$$
$$10 \text{ at } \$2.50 = \ 25.00$$
$$12 \text{ at } \$3.00 = \ 36.00$$
$$15 \text{ at } \$3.25 = \ 48.75$$
$$7 \text{ at } \$4.00 = \ 28.00$$

Cost of ending inventory = $147.75

Cost of goods sold

$$\$493.35$$
$$- \ 147.75$$
$$\$345.60$$

18-18. Complete the following (assume $90,000 of overhead to b distributed):

	Square feet	Ratio	Amount of overhead allocated
Department A	10,000	.25 (10,000 ÷ 40,000)	$22,500 (.25 × $90,000)

18-19.

	Square feet	Ratio	Amount of overhead allocated
Department B	30,000	.75 (30,000 ÷ 40,000)	$67,500 (.75 × $90,000)

Word Problems:

18-23. On January 30, 2009, Seneca Foods, from Marion, NY, announced the effect of LIFO on their inventory valuation method. Kraig H. Kayser, president and CEO, included a statement regarding inventory valuation. He stated: "Bottom-line performance has also been strong, notwithstanding the over doubling of the company's LIFO provision from $20.1 million to $41.9 million. The LIFO provision is a noncash adjustment to cost of goods that removes the inflationary impact on inventory costs." Assume Seneca purchased 25 units for $10.50 on January 1, 2008. On March 15, 2008, Seneca purchased an additional 15 units at $14.35. Finally, on November 30, 2008, 30 units were purchased at $15.75. Fifty units were sold. **(a)** What is the cost of ending inventory using LIFO? **(b)** What is the cost of merchandise sold using LIFO?

  a. Cost of ending inventory LIFO
    $25 \times \$10.50 = \$262.50$ Five sold, $45 + 5 = 50$; 20 remain
    $15 \times \$14.35 = \$215.25$ All sold: $30 + 15 = 45$
    $30 \times \$15.75 = \$472.50$ All sold: 30
             Total = $\$950.25$

    Cost of ending inventory: $20 \times \$10.50 = \$210.00$

  b. Cost of goods sold: $\$950.25 - \$210.00 = \$740.25$

18-27. Over the past 3 years, the gross profit rate for Jini Company was 35%. Last week a fire destroyed all Jini's inventory. Using the gross profit method, estimate the cost of inventory destroyed in the fire, given the following facts that were recorded in a fireproof safe:

		Goods available for sale	
Beginning inventory	$ 6,000	Beginning inventory	$ 6,000
Net purchases	$64,000	Net purchases	64,000
Net sales at retail	$49,000	Cost of goods available for sale	$70,000
		Less: Estimated cost of goods sold:	
		Net sales at retail	$49,000
		Cost percentage (100% − 35%)	.65
		Estimated cost of goods sold	31,850
		Estimated ending inventory	$38,150

18-29. Logan Company uses a perpetual inventory system on a FIFO basis. Assuming inventory on January 1 was 800 units at $8 each, what is the cost of ending inventory at the end of October 5?

Received			**Sold**		
Date	**Quantity**	**Cost per unit**	**Date**	**Quantity**	
Apr. 15	220	$5	Mar. 8	500	
Nov. 12	1,900	9	Oct. 5	200	
Jan. 1 inventory	$6,400	800 units at $8	Oct. 5 inventory	$1,900	100 units at $8
Mar. 8 inventory	2,400	300 units at $8			220 units at $5
Apr. 15 inventory	3,500	300 units at $8			
		220 units at $5			

CHAPTER 19 – Sales, Excise and Property Taxes

End–of–Chapter Problems

Drill Problems:

19-1. Calculate following:

Retail selling price		Sales tax (5%)		Excise tax (9%)	Total price including taxes
$800	+	$40 ($800 × .05)	+	$72 ($800 × .09)	$912

19-3. Calculate the actual sales since the sales and sales tax were rung up together, assume a 6% sales tax (round your answers to the nearest cent):

$$\frac{\$88,000}{1.06} = \$83,018.87$$

19-9. Complete the following:

Tax rate per dollar	In percent	Per $100	Per $1,000	Mills
.0 .0699	6.99% (.0699)	$6.99 (.0699 × 100)	$69.90 (.0699 × 1,000)	69.90 $\left(\dfrac{.0699}{.001}\right)$

Word Problems:

19-15. Don Chather bought a new Dell computer for $1,995. This included a 6% sales tax. What is the amount of sales tax and the selling price before the tax?

$\dfrac{\$1,995}{1.06} = \$1,882.08$ actual sale $1,995.00 - \$1,882.08 = \$112.92$ sales tax

19-21. Bill Shass pays a property tax of $3,200. In his community, the tax rate is 50 mills. What is Bill's assessed value?

Mills × .001 × A = $ 3,200
50 × .001 × A = $ 3,200
.05A = $ 3,200
A = $64,000

19-25. The property tax rate for Minneapolis is $8.73 per square foot, and the Denver rate is $2.14 a square foot. If 3,500 square feet is occupied at each location, what is the difference paid in property taxes?

$8.73 Minneapolis   3,500 square feet
− 2.14 Denver   × $6.59
$6.59 more of a square foot $23,065 more in Minneapolis

Challenge Problem:

19-27. Art Neuner, an investor in real estate, bought an office condominium. The market value of the condo was $250,000 with a 70% assessment rate. Art feels that his return should be 12% per month on his investment after all expenses. The tax rate is $31.50 per $1,000. Art estimates it will cost $275 per month to cover general repairs, insurance, and so on. He pays a $140 condo fee per month. All utilities and heat are the responsibility of the tenant. Calculate the monthly rent for Art. Round your answer to the nearest dollar (at intermediate stages).

$250,000 × .70 = $175,000 assessed value

Tax = 175 × $31.50 = $ 5,512.50 tax
+ 3,300.00 ($275 × 12) repairs and insurance
+ 1,680.00 ($140 × 12) condo fee

$10,492.50 ÷ 12 = $874 $874 × 1.12 = $978.88 = $979

CHAPTER 20 – Life, Fire and Auto Insurance

End–of–Chapter Problems

Drill Problems:

20-1. Calculate the annual premium for the following policies using Table 20.1 (for females subtract 3 years from the table).

Amount of coverage (face value of policy)	Age and sex of insured	Type of insurance policy	Annual premium
$70,000	35 F	Straight life	$70 \times \$9.71 = \$679.70$

20-7. Calculate the following no forfeiture options for Lee Chin, age 42, who purchased a $200,000 straight-life policy. At the end of year 20 Lee stopped paying premiums.

Option 3: Extended term insurance
21 years 300 days

20-9. Calculate the short-rate premium and refund of the following:

Annual premium	Canceled after	Short-rate premium	Refund
$700	8 months by insured	$518 (.74 × $700)	$182 ($700 − $518)

20-13. Calculate the annual auto insurance premium for the following:

Britney Sper, Territory 5
Class 17 operator
Compulsory, 10/20/5 $ 258 ($98 + $160)

Optional

a. Bodily injury, 500/1,000 $ 298

b. Property damage, 25M $ 166

c. Collision, $100 deductible $ 233 ($190 + $43)

   Age of car is 2; symbol of car is 7

d. Comprehensive, $200 deductible $ 112 ($108 + $4)

   Total annual premium $1,067

Word Problems:

20-19. Abby Ellen's toy store is worth $400,000 and is insured for $200,000. Assume an 80% coinsurance clause and that a fire caused $190,000 damage. What is the liability of the insurance company?

$$\frac{\$200,000}{\$320,000} \times \$190,000 = \$118,750 \qquad (.80 \times \$400,000)$$

20-21. As given via the Internet, auto insurance quotes gathered online could vary from $947 to $1,558. A class 18 operator carries compulsory 10/20/5 insurance. He has the following optional coverage: bodily injury, 500/1,000; property damage, 50M; and collision, $200 deductible. His car is 1 year old, and the symbol of the car is 8. He has comprehensive insurance with a $200 deductible. Using your text, what is the total annual premium?

Class 18 operator	
Compulsory, 10/20/5	$ 240 ($80 + $160)
Optional	
Bodily injury, 500/1,000	251
Property damage, 50M	168
Collision, $200 deductible	280 ($264 + $16)
Comprehensive, $200 deductible	161 ($157 + $4)
Total annual premium	$1,100

20-27. Marika Katz bought a new Blazer and insured it with only compulsory insurance 10/20/5. Driving up to her summer home one evening, Marika hit a parked car and injured the couple inside. Marika's car had damage of $7,500, and the car she struck had damage of $5,800. After a lengthy court suit, the couple struck were awarded personal injury judgments of $18,000 and $9,000, respectively. What will the insurance company pay for this accident, and what is Marika's responsibility?

Insurance company pays		Marika pays	
Bodily	$10,000 + $9,000	$ 8,000	
Property	5,000	7,500	no collision
		800	property damage not covered by compulsory
Total	$24,000	$16,300	

Challenge Problem:

20-29. Bill, who understands the types of insurance that are available, is planning his life insurance needs. At this stage of his life (age 35), he has budgeted $200 a year for life insurance premiums. Could you calculate for Bill the amount of coverage that is available under straight life and for a 5-year term? Could you also show Bill that if he were to die at age 40, how much more his beneficiary would receive if he'd been covered under the 5-year term? Round to the nearest thousand.

Straight life

$200 ÷ $11.26 = 17.762 × $1,000 = $17,762 = $18,000

Five-year term

$200 ÷ $2.23 = 89.686 × $1,000 = $89,686 = $90,000

$$\begin{array}{r} \$90,000 \\ -\ 18,000 \\ \hline \$72,000 \end{array}$$

CHAPTER 21 – Stocks, Bond and Mutual Funds

End–of–Chapter Problems

Drill Problems:

21-1.   Calculate the cost (omit commission) of buying the following shares of stock:

300 shares of Google at $382.99 $114,897   (300 × $382.99)

21-3.   Calculate the yield of each of the following stocks (round to the nearest tenth percent):

Company	Yearly dividend	Closing price per share	Yield
Boeing	$.68	$64.63	1.1% $\left(\dfrac{\$.68}{\$64.63}\right)$

21-5.   Calculate the earnings per share, price-earnings ratio (to nearest whole number), or stock price as needed:

Company	Earnings per share	Closing price per share	Price-earnings ratio
BellSouth	$3.15	$40.13	13 $\left(\dfrac{\$40.13}{\$3.15}\right)$

21-7.   Calculate the total cost of buying 400 shares of CVS at $59.38. Assume a 2% commission.
400 shares × $59.38 = $23,752 × 1.02 = $24,227.04

21-9.   Given: 20,000 shares cumulative preferred stock ($2.25 dividend per share): 40,000 shares common stock. Dividends paid: 2010, $8,000; 2011, 0; and 2012, $160,000. How much will preferred and common receive each year?

Year	2010	2011	2012
Dividend paid	$8,000	–0–	$160,000
Preferred	$8,000	–0–	$37,000 + $45,000
	($37,000)	($45,000)	+ $45,000 = $127,000
Common	–0–	–0–	$160,000 – $127,000
			= $33,000

21-13. For the following bonds, calculate the total annual interest, total cost, and current yield (to the nearest tenth percent):

Wang 6½   14   4   68.125 $260.00 $2,725   9.5%

.065 × $1,000 = $65 $\dfrac{\$65}{\$681.25}$ (.68125 × $1,000)

interest per bond

56

Word Problems:

21-21. The following bond was quoted in the *Wall Street Journal*:

Bonds	Curr. yld.	Vol.	Close	Net chg.
NY Tel $7\frac{1}{4}$ 11	7.2	10	100.875	$+1\frac{1}{8}$

Five bonds were purchased yesterday, and 5 bonds were purchased today. How much more did the 5 bonds cost today (in dollars)?

Today: $5 \times \$1,008.75$ $(1.00875 \times \$1,000) = \$5,043.75$

Yesterday:
$$
\begin{array}{r}
100.875 \\
-\ 1.125 \\
\hline
99.75
\end{array}
$$

$5 \times \$997.50$ $(.9975 \times 1,000) =$
$$
\begin{array}{r}
-\ 4,987.50 \\
\hline
\$\quad 56.25
\end{array}
$$

21-23. Ron bought a bond of Bee Company for 79.25. The original bond was $5\frac{3}{4}$ 12. Ron wants to know the current yield (to the nearest tenth percent). Please help Ron with the calculation.

$.7925 \times \$1,000 = \$792.50$

$\dfrac{\$57.50}{\$792.50} = 7.3\%$ $\qquad (5\frac{3}{4}\% = 5.75\% = .0575 \times \$1,000 = \$57.50)$

21-29. Ron and Madeleine Couple received their 2010 Form 1099-DIV (dividends received) in the amount of $1,585. Ron and Madeleine are in the 28% bracket. What would be their tax liability on the dividends received?

$$
\begin{array}{r}
\$\ 1,585 \text{ dividends received} \\
\times \quad .28 \text{ (tax bracket)} \\
\hline
\$443.80
\end{array}
$$

21-31. On September 6, Irene Westing purchased one bond of Mick Corporation at 98.50. The bond pays $8\frac{3}{4}$ interest on June 1 and December 1. The stockbroker told Irene that she would have to pay the accrued interest and the market price of the bond and a $6 brokerage fee. What was the total purchase price for Irene? Assume a 360-day year (each month is 30 days) in calculating the accrued interest. (*Hint:* Final cost = Cost of bond + Accrued interest + Brokerage fee. Calculate time for accrued interest.)

Cost of bond: $\$1,000 \times .985 = \$985$

Time for accrued interest:

June	30 days
July	30 days
August	30 days
September	6 days
	96 days

Interest: $\$1,000 \times .0875 = \$87.50$

$\dfrac{\$87.50}{360} = \$.2430555$ per day

$$
\begin{array}{r}
\times \qquad 96 \\
\hline
\$\quad 23.33
\end{array}
$$

Final cost of bond	$ 985.00
Accrued interest	23.33
Brokerage fee	6.00
	$1,014.33

CHAPTER 22 – Business Statistics

End–of–Chapter Problems

Drill Problems:

22-1. Calculate the mean (to the nearest hundredth):

$$12, 9, 8, 3 = \frac{32}{4} = 8.00$$

22-7. Find the median:

$$55, 10, 19, 38, 100, 25 \quad \frac{25 + 38}{2} = 31.5$$
$$10, 19, 25, 38, 55, 100$$

22-11. **Given:**

Truck cost	2012	$30,000
Truck cost	2008	$21,000

Calculate the price relative (round to the nearest tenth percent).

$$\frac{\$30,000}{\$21,000} \times 100 = 142.9$$

22-15. How many degrees on a pie chart would each be given from the following?

Wear digital watch	42%	$.42 \times 360° = 151.2°$
Wear traditional watch	51%	$.51 \times 360° = 183.6°$
Wear no watch	7%	$.07 \times 360° = \underline{25.2°}$
		$360°$

Word Problems:

22-17. The American Kennel Club posted a list of the most popular purebred dogs in the United States on January 21, 2009. Labrador Retrievers hold the number-one spot again for the 18th consecutive year. Twice as many Labs were registered last year than any other breed. Angela Newman's dog club has the following dogs as members: 35 Labrador Retrievers, 15 Yorkshire Terriers, 12 German Shepherds, 10 Golden Retrievers, 8 Beagles, and 6 Boxers. Create a pie chart showing these statistics.

$35 + 15 + 12 + 10 + 8 + 6 = 86$

$35 \div 86 = 0.41 \times 360° = 147.6°$
$15 \div 86 = 0.17 \times 360° = 61.2°$
$12 \div 86 = 0.14 \times 360° = 50.4°$
$10 \div 86 = 0.12 \times 360° = 43.2°$
$8 \div 86 = 0.09 \times 360° = 32.4°$
$6 \div 86 = 0.07 \times 360° = \underline{25.2°}$
Total: 360.0°

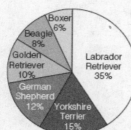

22-19. Bill Small, a travel agent, provided Alice Hall with the following information regarding the cost of her upcoming vacation:

Transportation	35%
Hotel	28%
Food and entertainment	20%
Miscellaneous	17%

Construct a circle graph for Alice.

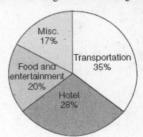

$.35 \times 360° = 126°$

$.28 \times 360° = 100.8°$

$.20 \times 360° = 72°$

$.17 \times 360° = 61.2°$

22-22. Melvin Company reported sales in 2011 of $300,000. This compared to sales of $150,000 in 2010 and $100,000 in 2009. Construct a line graph for Melvin Company.

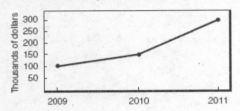

Challenge Problem:

22-23. Mortgage rates have fluctuated greatly over the past 20 years. Prepare a frequency distribution of the following 30-year fixed-rate mortgage rates from Freddie Mac. Calculate the mean, median, mode, range, and standard deviation. Round to the nearest hundredth. Is this a normal distribution?

Year	Rate	Year	Rate	Year	Rate	Year	Rate
1990	10.13	1995	7.93	2000	8.05	2005	5.87
1991	9.25	1996	7.81	2001	6.97	2006	6.41
1992	8.39	1997	7.60	2002	6.54	2007	6.34
1993	7.31	1998	6.94	2003	5.83	2008	6.03
1994	8.38	1999	7.44	2004	5.84	2009	5.07 est.

Use the following intervals for the frequency distribution:

	Tally	Frequency
5.00–6.0	IIII	4
6.01–7.0	JHHI I	6
7.01–8.0	JHHI	5
8.01–9.0	III	3
9.01–10.0	I	1
10.01–11.0	I	1

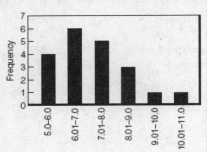

Mean:
$$\frac{10.13 + 7.93 + 8.05 + 5.87 + 9.25 + 7.81 + 6.97 + 6.41 + 8.39 + 7.60 + 6.54 + 6.34 + 7.31 + 6.94 + 5.83 + 6.03 + 8.38 + 7.44 + 5.84 + 5.07}{20}$$

$144.16 \div 20 = 7.208 = 7.21$

Median: 5.07 5.83 5.84 5.87 6.03 6.34 6.41 6.54 6.94 6.97 7.31 7.44
7.60 7.81 7.91 8.08 8.38 8.39 9.25 10.13

Middle numbers: $\frac{6.97 + 7.31}{2} = 7.14$

Mode: N/A

Range: $10.13 - 5.07 = 5.06$

CHAPTER 1

Self-Paced Worksheet

Cover the answers on the right and fill in each blank. After answering the question, look to the right for your answer.

Vocabulary Review

1. The _____ _____ place-value chart divides groups of three digits right to left by units, thousands, millions, billions, and trillions.
2. The total in the adding process is called the _____.
3. The smaller number that is being subtracted from another is called the _____.
4. The answer from a subtraction problem is the _____.
5. Numbers that are combined in the addition process are called _____.
6. Multiplicand times multiplier equals the _____.
7. The _____ is the number in the division process that is dividing into another.
8. The _____ is the leftover amount in the division process.
9. _____ _____ _____ _____ results in only one nonzero digit left. This means rounding to first digit of number.
10. The _____ is the answer of a division problem.

1. whole number
2. sum
3. subtrahend
4. difference
5. addends
6. product
7. divisor
8. remainder
9. rounding all the way
10. quotient

Theory Tips (and/or Cautions)

11. The 5 in 7,853 is in the _____ place.
12. The 4 in 64,115,328 is in the _____ place.
13. In rounding 1,456 to the nearest thousands, the first step is to identify the _____ _____ of the digit you want to round.
14. In rounding, if digit to right of identified digit is _____ or greater, identified digit is increased by one.
15. Rounding all the way results in only _____ _____ digit remaining.
16. The first step in dissecting a word problem is to _____ _____ _____.
17. Adding of whole numbers is done _____ to _____.
18. The difference plus the subtrahend equals the _____.
19. The numbers between the multiplier and the product are _____ _____.
20. We can _____ the multiplication process by reversing the multiplicand and multiplier and then multiplying.
21. 75,000 × 20 is completed by multiplying 75 × 2 and _____ _____ zeros to answer.
22. The divisor times quotient plus remainder equals the _____.
23. 66,000 ÷ 100 results in dropping _____ zeros in the dividend.

11. tens
12. millions
13. place value
14. five
15. one nonzero
16. gather the facts
17. top bottom
18. minuend
19. partial products
20. check
21. adding (affixing) four
22. dividend
23. two

Calculations/Applications

Do calculations on scrap paper as needed. Worked-out solutions are provided at end.

24. Write in verbal the whole number 8,593 and illustrate place values.

24. eight thousand, five hundred ninety-three
(8 × 1,000) + (5 × 100) + (9 × 10) + (3 × 1)

25. Round 9,852 to nearest hundred.
26. Round 62,555 to nearest thousand.
27. Round 6,853 all the way.
28. Estimate by rounding all the way and then do actual calculation.
6,666
7,500
7,215

25. 9,900
26. 63,000
27. 7,000
28. 22,000 est. 21,381

29. Subtract: 9,432
　　　　　 −3,618

30. Multiply 86 × 1,000 by the shortcut method.

31. Multiply 751 (do not multiply rows of zeros).
　　　　406

32. Divide 7,041 ÷ 128 and show any remainder.

33. Divide 99,000 ÷ 100 by the shortcut method.

34. Chrysler produces 650 vans each workday (Monday through Friday). If the cost to produce each car is $7,000, what is Chrysler's cost for the year?

Worked-Out Solutions to Calculations/Applications Section

25. 9,852 → 9,900
　　　　↑

26. 62,555 → 63,000
　　　　↑

27. 6,853 → 7,000
　　　　↑

28. 6,666 → 7,000
　　　 7,500 → 8,000
　　　 7,215 → 7,000
　　　 21,381　22,000

29. 8 14 2 12
　　　 9,4 3 2
　　　 3, 6 1 8
　　　 5, 8 1 4

30. 86 + 3 zeros

31. 751
　　　 406
　　　 4506
　　　30040
　　304,906

32. 　　55 Rem1
　　128)7041
　　　　640
　　　　641
　　　　640
　　　　　1

33. 99,000 = 990

34. 　　　　 5 × 650 = 3,250
　　　　 3,250 × 52 = 169,000
　　169,000 × $7,000 = $1,183,000,000

Word Problem Practice Quiz

Check with your instructor for complete worked-out solutions.

1–1. Mel Jones received the following grades in a computer science class: 90, 70, 50, 85, 75, and 60. The instructor said he would drop the lowest grade. What is Mel's average?

1–2. Judy Small had a $850 balance in her checkbook. During the week, she wrote checks for rent, $180; telephone, $60; food, $95; and entertaining $45. She also made a deposit of $1,200. Calculate the new checkbook balance.

1–3. James Company carpeted its offices requiring 711 square yards of commercial carpet. The total cost of the carpet was $3,555. How much did James pay per square yard?

1–4. The Angel Company produced 26,580 cans of paint in August. Angel was able to sell 21,946 of these cans. Calculate ending inventory of paint cans along with its total inventory cost assuming each can cost $12.

1–5. A computer with a regular price of $4,500 was reduced by $1,255. Calculate the new selling price of the computer. Assuming 900 customers purchased the computer, what were the sales to the store?

1–6. Mills Hardware on Monday sold 40 rakes at $7 each, 8 wrenches at $5 each, 10 bags of grass seed at $6 each, 9 lawn mowers at $205 each, and 33 cans of paint at $4 each. What were the total dollar sales for Mills on Monday?

1–7. Dick Herch, a college editor, was going on a business trip that would take him from Boston (starting point) to New York and to Washington, D.C. Dick estimated he would be traveling 1,901 miles round trip. In actuality, the drive from Boston to New York was 228 miles, and from New York to Washington, D.C. was 242 miles. Calculate how many miles Dick overestimated his trip.

1–8. Jay Miller loves to ski. He rents a ski chalet for $1,350 per month for 4 months. What is Jay's rental charge for the 4 months? Assume Jay spends $6,250 for the total trip. How much did he spend above the renting of the ski chalet?

1–9. Jill Rite borrowed $20,000 to buy a new car. Assume a finance charge of $4,900. What will be her monthly payment if she takes 60 months to repay the loan (plus finance charge)? Assume the loan is repaid in equal payments.

1–10. Jim Rose bought 7,000 shares of stock in the Flight Company. After holding the stock for 6 months, he sold 400 shares on Monday, 330 shares on Tuesday and again on Thursday, and 800 shares on Friday. Calculate the total number of shares Jim still has. If the average share of stock is worth $39 per share, what is the total value of his stock?

CHAPTER 2

Self-Paced Worksheet

Cover the answers on the right and fill in each blank. After answering the question, look to the right for your answer.

Vocabulary Review

1. Like fractions are _____ _____ with the same denominators.
2. _____ is the reducing process to simplify multiplication and division of fractions.
3. A fraction reaches its _____ _____ when no number divides evenly into the numerator and denominator except the number 1.
4. $\frac{7}{5}$, of which 5 is called the _____.
5. A _____ _____ (larger than 1) is only divisible by itself and one.
6. The _____ _____ _____ is the smallest nonzero whole number into which all denominators will divide evenly.
7. The _____ _____ _____ is the largest possible number that will divide evenly into both the numerator and denominator.
8. The _____ of a fraction is the interchanging of the numerator and denominator.
9. An _____ _____ is when the numerator is equal to or greater than the denominator.
10. _____ _____ are proper fractions with different denominators.

1.	proper fractions
2.	cancellation
3.	lowest terms
4.	denominator
5.	prime number
6.	least common denominator
7.	greatest common divisor
8.	reciprocal
9.	improper fraction
10.	unlike fractions

Theory Tips (and/or Cautions)

11. When converting an improper fraction to a mixed number, the remainder will be placed over the _____ denominator.
12. When converting mixed numbers to improper fractions, the _____ will stay the same.
13. The greatest common divisor cannot be a _____.
14. Dividing numerator and denominator by the greatest common divisor will result in reducing the fraction to its _____ _____.
15. The _____ _____ you use is the greatest common divisor when using the step approach.
16. $\frac{2}{7}$ or $\frac{8}{28}$ are _____ in value.
17. In adding or subtracting fractions, they should be _____ _____ _____ terms.
18. In adding or subtracting fractions with different denominators, the _____ _____ _____ must be found.
19. In finding the LCD by prime numbers, the next highest prime number will be used if smaller prime number will not divide evenly into at least _____ numbers.
20. When borrowing _____ from a whole number where subtracting in a mixed number problem, it has the same value as $\frac{5}{5}$ or $\frac{4}{4}$.
21. $\frac{4}{1}$ is equal to _____.
22. If cancellation is not used in the multiplying of mixed numbers the answer may have to be _____ _____ _____ _____.
23. 5 and $\frac{1}{5}$ are _____. When these two numbers are multiplied, they equal 1.
24. If your answer is an _____ _____ be sure to reduce it to lowest terms.

11.	old
12.	denominator
13.	zero
14.	lowest terms
15.	last divisor
16.	equivalent
17.	reduced to lowest
18.	least common denominator
19.	two
20.	1
21.	4
22.	reduced to lowest terms
23.	reciprocals
24.	improper fraction

Calculations/Applications

Do calculations on scrap paper as needed. Worked-out solutions are provided at end.

25. Convert to mixed number: $\frac{150}{7}$
26. Convert to an improper fraction: $9\frac{5}{8}$
27. Find the GCD by step approach and reduce to lowest terms: $\frac{15}{80}$
28. Convert to higher terms: $\frac{7}{10} = \frac{}{90}$

25.	$21\frac{3}{7}$
26.	$\frac{77}{8}$
27.	$5; \frac{3}{16}$
28.	$\frac{63}{90}$

29. Find the LCD: 15 6 3 4 2

30. Subtract: $8\frac{1}{8} - 6\frac{7}{24}$

31. Multiply (use cancelling): $14 \times \frac{2}{7}$

32. Multiply (do not use cancelling; reduce by GCD): $\frac{7}{8} \times \frac{6}{9}$

33. Complete: $\frac{1}{4} \div \frac{3}{6}$

34. A recent testing survey showed $\frac{1}{4}$ of all people surveyed preferred baking soda toothpaste to regular. If 26,000 people were in the survey, how many favored regular toothpaste? How many favored baking soda toothpaste?

Worked-Out Solutions to Calculations/Applications Section

25.
$$7)\overline{150} = 21\frac{3}{7}$$
$$\begin{array}{r} 21 \\ \hline 14 \\ \hline 10 \\ 7 \\ \hline 3 \end{array}$$

26. $9\frac{5}{8} = \frac{72 + 5}{8} = \frac{77}{8}$

27.
$$15)\overline{80} \quad \textcircled{5})\overline{15} \quad \frac{15 \div 5}{80 \div 5} = \frac{3}{16}$$
$$\begin{array}{r} 5 \\ \hline 75 \\ \hline 5 \end{array} \quad \begin{array}{r} 3 \\ \hline 15 \end{array}$$

28. $\frac{7}{10} = \frac{63}{90} \leftarrow (9 \times 7)$

29.
$$\begin{array}{c|ccccc} 2 & 15 & 6 & 3 & 4 & 2 \\ \hline 3 & 15 & 3 & 3 & 2 & 1 \\ \hline & 5 & 1 & 1 & 2 & 1 \end{array}$$
$$2 \times 3 \times 5 \times 1 \times 1 \times 2 \times 1 = 60$$

30.
$$\begin{aligned} 8\frac{1}{8} &= 8\frac{3}{24} = 7\frac{27}{24} \\ -6\frac{7}{24} &- 6\frac{7}{24} = 6\frac{7}{24} \\ \hline &= 1\frac{20}{24} = 1\frac{5}{6} \end{aligned}$$

31. $\overset{2}{\cancel{14}} \times \frac{2}{\cancel{7}} = 4$
$_{1}$

32. $\frac{7}{8} \times \frac{6}{9} = \frac{42}{72}$

$$42)\overline{72} \quad 30)\overline{42} \quad 12)\overline{30} \quad 6)\overline{12}$$
$$\begin{array}{r} 1 \\ \hline 42 \\ \hline 30 \end{array} \quad \begin{array}{r} 1 \\ \hline 30 \\ \hline 12 \end{array} \quad \begin{array}{r} 2 \\ \hline 24 \\ \hline 6 \end{array} \quad \begin{array}{r} 2 \\ \hline 12 \end{array}$$

$$\frac{42 \div 6}{72 \div 6} = \frac{7}{12}$$

33. $\frac{1}{\underset{2}{\cancel{4}}} \times \frac{\overset{3}{\cancel{6}}}{\underset{1}{\cancel{3}}} = \frac{1}{2}$

34. $\frac{3}{4} \times 26,000 = 19,500$

$\frac{1}{4} \times 26,000 = 6,500$

Word Problem Practice Quiz

Check with your instructor for complete worked-out solutions.

2–1. A survey conducted by a marketing class found that $\frac{7}{8}$ of all people surveyed favored digital watches over traditional styles. If 3,200 responded to the survey, how many actually favored using traditional watches?

2–2. Jack, Alice, and Frank entered into a partnership. Jack owns $\frac{1}{5}$ of the company and Alice owns $\frac{1}{8}$. Calculate what part is owned by Frank.

2–3. Bob Campbell, who loves to cook, makes an apple pie (serves 6) for his family. The recipe calls for $3\frac{1}{2}$ cups of apples, $2\frac{3}{4}$ cups of flour, $\frac{1}{8}$ cup of margarine, $2\frac{1}{8}$ cups of sugar, and 5 eggs. Since guests are coming, he would like to make this pie to serve 24. How much of each ingredient should Bob use?

2–4. A trip from Boston to the White Mountains of New Hampshire will take $2\frac{7}{8}$ hours. Assume we are $\frac{1}{7}$ of the way there. How much longer will the trip take?

2–5. The price of a new van has increased by $\frac{2}{5}$. If the original price of the van was $15,000, what is the new price today?

2–6. Jim Smith felled a tree that was 120 feet long. Jim decided to cut the tree into pieces of $2\frac{1}{2}$ feet. How many pieces can be cut from this tree?

2–7. JHS Company's stock on Monday reached a high of $\$99\frac{1}{8}$ per share. At the end of the day the stock plummeted to $\$68\frac{5}{8}$. How much did the stock fall from its high on Monday?

2–8. During the winter, Bill Blank has been quite concerned about the total number of gallons of home heating fuel he used. Last winter he used $1,505\frac{7}{8}$ gallons of oil. Here is a summary of this year's usage. Is it more or less than the previous year? Also, how much more or less?

December	$525\frac{1}{4}$	February	$481\frac{3}{8}$
January	$488\frac{5}{8}$	March	$255\frac{1}{3}$

2–9. John Toby is paid $70 per day. John became ill on Monday and had to leave after $\frac{3}{7}$ of a day. What did he earn on Monday? (Assume no work, no pay).

2–10. Evan Summers bought $1\frac{3}{8}$ pounds of roast beef, $4\frac{5}{7}$ pounds of sliced cheese, and $\frac{3}{5}$ of a pound of coleslaw. What is the total weight of his purchases?

CHAPTER 3

Self-Paced Worksheet

Cover the answers on the right and fill in each blank. After answering the question, look to the right for your answer.

Vocabulary Review

1. The position located between units and tenths is called the _____ _____.
2. _____ are numbers written with digits to right of the decimal point.
3. A _____ _____ is a fraction with a denominator that has a power of 10.
4. A _____ _____ has no whole number(s) to left of the decimal point.
5. A _____ _____ is a combination of a whole number and a decimal.
6. Decimal numbers that repeat themselves continuously are called _____ _____.

1. decimal point
2. decimals
3. decimal fraction
4. pure decimal
5. mixed decimal
6. repeating decimals

Theory Tips (and/or Cautions)

7. 4.53918   The 1 is in the _____ _____ place value.
8. In rounding decimals, drop _____ _____ to right of the identified digit.
9. .8, .80, .800 all have the same _____.
10. .33$\overline{3}$ is an example of a _____ decimal.
11. 3.0, 3.000, 3.0000 all have the same _____.
12. If the total number of places is greater than there are places in the product (from multiplying decimals), insert _____ in front of the product.
13. The _____ does not change when we multiply the divisor and dividend by the same number.
14. When multiplying decimals by multiples of 10, the answers are _____ than the original number.
15. When dividing decimals by multiples of 10, the answers are _____ than the original number.

7. ten thousandths
8. all digits
9. value
10. repeating
11. value
12. zeros

13 quotient

14. larger

15. smaller

Calculations/Applications

Do calculations on scrap paper as needed. Worked-out solutions are provided at end.

16. .3333 rounded to nearest thousandths is _____.
17. .16593 rounded to nearest hundredth is _____.
18. Convert to a decimal: $\frac{88}{100,000}$
19. .713 converted to a decimal fraction is _____.
20. .07$\frac{1}{4}$ converted to a decimal fraction is _____.
21. $\frac{1}{6}$ converted to decimal is _____ (round to nearest hundredth).
22. Rearrange vertically and add: 4.1, 14.82, 16.321
23. Multiply and round to nearest hundredth: 15.41 × 18.8
24. Divide and round to nearest hundredth: 3,142 ÷ 3.91
25. Complete by shortcut method: 4,138 ÷ 10,000
26. At Hertz, the cost per day to rent a full-size car is $49.99, plus $.18 per mile. What is the charge to rent this car for 2 days if you drove 959.8 miles?
27. A $2,800 computer would cost how much in Canada? (Use table in *Business Math Handbook;* round to nearest cent.)

16. .333
17. .17
18. .00088
19. $\frac{713}{1,000}$
20. $\frac{725}{10,000}$
21. .17
22. 35.241
23. 289.71
24. 803.58
25. .4138
26. $272.74

27. $4,023.32

Worked-Out Solutions to Calculations/Applications Section

16. .33$\underset{\uparrow}{3}$3 → .333

17. .1$\underset{\uparrow}{6}$593 → .17

18. $\frac{88}{100,000}$ ← .00088 5 places

19. $\frac{713}{1,000}$ (1 + 3 places)

20. $.07\frac{1}{4} \rightarrow$ .07

             $+.0025$

          $.0725 \rightarrow \dfrac{725}{1 + 4 \text{ places}} = \dfrac{725}{10,000}$

21. $\dfrac{1}{6} = .166 = .17$
          $\uparrow$

22.
     4.100
   14.820
   16.321
   35.241

23.
```
    1 5.4 1
  × 1 8.8
    1 2 3 2 8
    1 2 3 2 8
    1 5 4 1
  2 8 9 7 0 8 → 289.708 → 289.71
                    ↑
```

24.
```
         803.580
3.91 )314200.000 → 803.58
      3128
      1400
      1173
      2270
      1955
      3150
      3128
       220
```

25. $.4138 \rightarrow .4138$

26. $\$49.99 \times 2 \;\; = \$\;99.98$

     $\$.18 \times 959.8 = \underline{\;172.76}$

     Total charge $= \$272.74$

27. $\$2,800 \times 1.4369 = \$4,023.32$

Word Problem Practice Quiz

Check with your instructor for complete worked-out solutions.

Round where applicable to nearest hundredth.

3–1. Bob Baker bought season tickets to a professional basketball team's games. The cost was $795.88. The package included 38 home games. What is the average price of the tickets per game? Round to nearest cent. Jim has requested to buy 4 of the tickets from Bob. What will be the total price Bob should receive?

3–2. The level of the oil tank in Henry's basement at the beginning of January read 310.75 gallons. During the month it was filled with 112.85 gallons. Henry used 125.95 gallons in January. What is the number of gallons of oil that Henry has to begin February?

3–3. Printed pencils cost $.08\overline{3}$ each for an order of 144,000 pencils. On Monday, Jim Company placed an order for the 144,000 pencils. What is the cost of the pencils for Jim Company? (Hint: Use the fractional equivalent in your calculation.)

3–4. Irene was shopping for corn beef at Market A; it was $2.158 per pound. At Market B, corn beef was $2.06 per pound. How much cheaper is Market B?

3–5. Shelley Scupper bought a new sweater for $101.88. She gave the salesperson two $100 bills. what is Shelley's change?

3–6. Joe is traveling to a convention by car. His company will reimburse him $.34 per mile.

Assume Joe traveled 1,011.8 miles. What reimbursement can he expect?

3–7. Morris Katz bought 4 new tires for his car at $129.35 per tire. He was also charged $3.15 per tire for mounting, $2.80 per tire for valve cores, and $4.95 per tire for balancing. Assuming no tax, what did Morris really pay for those 4 tires?

3–8. Alice wants to put wall-to-wall carpeting in her house. She will need 108.7 yards for downstairs, 19.8 yards for halls, and 175.9 yards for the upstairs bedrooms. She chose a shag carpet that costs $14.95 per yard. Alice also ordered foam padding at $3.25 per year. The installers quoted Alice a labor cost of $6.10 per yard in installation. What will the total job cost Alice?

3–9. A trip to Mexico costs 4,900 pesos. How much would this be in U.S. dollars? Check your answer.

3–10. The normal winter snowfall is 129.55 inches for Jordan County. this winter, the following snowfall resulted:

	Inches
December	29.33
January	44.453
February	18.85
March	16.35

What was this winter's total snowfall? How much was the snowfall above or below normal?

CHAPTER 4

Self-Paced Worksheet

Cover the answers on the right and fill in each blank. After answering the question, look to the right for your answer.

Vocabulary Review:

1. _____ _____ is the process of comparing the bank balance to the checkbook balance.

2. A record-keeping device called a _____ _____ records checks paid and deposits made by companies using a checking account.

3. A _____ _____ provides a record of checks written.

4. A _____ _____ identifies the next person or company to whom the check is to be transferred.

5. The _____ is the one who is named to receive the amount of the check.

6. Credit card sales less returns equal _____ _____.

7. A _____ memo indicates what a bank is adding to your account.

8. One who writes the check is called the _____.

9. _____ _____ _____ are deposits not received or processed by the bank at the time the bank statement is prepared.

10. Checks written but not yet processed by the bank before the bank statement preparation are called _____ _____.

1.	bank reconciliation
2.	check register
3.	check stub
4.	full endorsement
5.	payee
6.	net deposits
7.	credit
8.	drawer
9.	deposits in transit
10.	outstanding checkts

Theory Tips (and/or Cautions)

11. If the verbal amount on a check doesn't match the figure amount, the bank by law uses the _____ amount.

12. _____ _____ can be further endorsed by someone who receives it intentionally or through loss.

13. A _____ _____ means the bank is decreasing one's account.

14. _____ is an important cause of differences between bank and checkbook.

15. An NSF will result in the bank _____ one's checkbook balance.

16. In the reconciliation process, deposits in transit and outstanding checks affect the _____ balance.

17. If the bank statement shows a note collected, the checkbook balance in the reconciliation process will be _____.

18. If a $20 check was recorded as $10, we need to lower the _____ balance by another $10.

19. Interest earned on a checking account will be _____ to one's account.

20. ATM cards are _____ cards.

21. Check stubs should be _____ before the check is written.

11.	verbal
12.	blank endorsement
13.	debit memorandum
14.	timing
15.	lowering
16.	bank
17.	increased
18.	checkbook
19.	credited
20.	debit
21.	completed

Calculations/Applications

Do calculations on scrap paper as needed. Worked-out solutions are provided at end.

22. Given the following from the check register, calculate the ending balance.

Beginning balance		$481.92
Payment	$ 81.22	
Payment	19.44	
Deposit	111.22	
Payment	88.04	

22. $404.44

68

23. Write the following amount in verbal form as you would on a check: $675.88

24. Calculate reconciled bank balance, given the following:

Bank statement balance	$4,800.10
Checks outstanding	55.32
Deposits in transit	105.99

25. Calculate reconciled checkbook balance, given the following:

Checkbook balance	$4,511.20
Interest earned	15.10
Note collected	555.10
ATM withdrawal	66.90
NSF check	12.55

26. Calculate a reconciled balance from the following:

Checkbook balance	$2,885
Bank balance	2,999
Interest earned	22
Deposits in transit	500
Checks outstanding	620
NSF check	15
Check printing	13

27. Angel's checkbook balance was $9,000. The bank statement had a balance of $10,500. Angel's bookkeeper noticed checks No. 140 for $550 and No. 145 for $205 were not yet processed by the bank. Angel made a deposit of $1,200 that had not reached the bank before preparation of the bank statement. Bank service charges totaled $40. The statement showed that the bank collected a note from Angel for $2,020 charging a $20 collection fee. Angel's bookkeeper noticed that a check for $30 was recorded as $15. What is the reconciled balance?

Worked-Out Solutions to Calculations/Applications Section

22. $481.92 − $81.22 − $19.44 + $111.22 − $88.04 = $404.44

24. $4,800.10 − $55.32 + $105.99 = $4,850.77

25.
$$
\begin{array}{r}
\$4,511.20 \\
+\ 15.10 \\
+\ 555.10 \\
-\ 66.90 \\
-\ 12.55 \\
\hline
\$5,001.95
\end{array}
$$

26.
$$
\begin{array}{ll}
\$2,885 & \\
+\ 22 & \$2,999 \\
-\ 15 & +\ 500 \\
-\ 13 & -\ 620 \\
\hline
\$2,879 & \$2,879
\end{array}
$$

27.

Checkbook

Angel's checkbook balance	$ 9,000
Add:	
Collection of note (less fee)	2,000
	$11,000
Deduct:	
Bank service charge: $40	
Book error 15	55
Reconciled balance	$10,945

Bank

Bank balance	$10,500
Add:	
Deposits in transit	1,200
	$11,700
Deduct:	
Outstanding checks:	
No. 140 $550	
No. 145 205	755
Reconciled balance	$10,945

Word Problem Practice Quiz

Check with your instructor for complete worked-out solutions.

4–1. Jones Bank sent a bank statement to Venice Company showing an ending balance of $1,900.00. There was a service charge of $9.00 on the bank statement. The bookkeeper of Venice Company noticed in the reconciliation process a deposit in transit of $850 along with checks outstanding of $300. Complete the reconciliation for Venice assuming a beginning balance of $2,459.

4–2. Al Ring received his bank statement from Jones Bank indicating a balance of $1,751.88. Ring's checkbook showed a balance of $1,512.70. Al noticed that a check for $261.18 was outstanding. The bank statement also revealed a NSF check for $12.00 and a service charge of $10.00. Reconcile this bank statement for Al.

4–3. The Bank statement for Janet Company revealed a balance of $2,585.22, while the checkbook balance showed $2,345.84. Checks for $116.55 and $129.33 were outstanding. A check printing charge for $6.50 was on the bank statement. Prepare a bank reconciliation.

4–4. The checkbook balance of Jeep Company showed a balance of $10,636.15. The bank statement showed a balance of $9,750.44. Checks outstanding totaled $2,850.11. There was a deposit in transit of $3,525.32 along with a NSF notice for $225.00. Jeep Company had earned interest of $14.50 of its checking account. Prepare a bank reconciliation.

4–5. The checkbook of Moore Company showed a balance of $5,844.61. The bank statement revealed a balance of $6,950.11. Check Nos. 59 and 68 were outstanding for $750 and $219, respectively. A deposit for $435 was not listed on the bank statement. The bank collected a $600 note for Moore. Check charges for the month were $28.50. Prepare a bank reconciliation.

4–6. The checkbook balance of Roe Company is $7,069.77. The bank statement reveals a balance of $3,940.11. The bank statement showed interest earned of $24, and a service charge of $15.10. There is a deposit in transit of $6,850.44. Outstanding checks totaled $1,911.88. The bookkeeper in further analyzing the bank statement noticed a collection of a note by bank for $3,000. Roe Company forgot to deduct a check for $1,200 during the month. Prepare a bank reconciliation.

4–7. The bank statement of May 31 for Jay Company showed a balance of $6,600.11. The bookkeeper of Jay Company noticed from the bank statement that the bank had collected a note for $1,500.00. There was a deposit in transit that Jay Company made on June 1 for $5,008.10, along with the outstanding checks of $2,210.11. Check charges were $52.00. Assist the bookkeeper of Jay in preparing a reconciled statement. Assume the checkbook balance of Jay equals to $7,950.10.

4–8. On December 31, the checkbook balance of Rose Company was $8,437.00. The bank statement balance showed $9,151.88. Checks outstanding totaled $1,341.88. The statement revealed a deposit in transit of $610.55, as well as a check charge of $11.80. The company earned interest income of $7.50 that was shown on the report. The bookkeeper forgot to record a check for $12.15. Complete a bank reconciliation for Rose.

4–9. Skol's checkbook currently has a balance of $12,280.56. The bank statement shows a balance of $8,915.33. The statement revealed interest income of $27.00, along with check charges of $18.10. Skol recorded a $115 check as $100. Deposits in transit were $5,811.44. Check Nos. 85, 88, and 92 for $800.11, $700.88, and $951.32 were not returned with the statement. Prepare a bank reconciliation for Skol.

CHAPTER 5

Self-Paced Worksheet

Cover the answers on the right and fill in each blank. After answering the question, look to the right for your answer.

Vocabulary Review

1. A number such as 4 or -8 is called a _____.
2. An _____ is a math statement that shows equality for expressions or numbers or both.
3. A _____ is an equation that expresses in symbols a fact, rule, or principle.
4. _____ and _____ are terms of mathematical expressions.
5. The variable we are solving for is called an _____.
6. _____ are letters or symbols that represent unknowns.

1.	constant
2.	equation
3.	formula
4.	constants, variables
5.	unknown
6.	variables

Theory Tips (and/or Cautions)

7. The letter _____ could be a variable or confused with multiplication.
8. Constants have a _____ value.
9. If a variable has no number in front of it, it is assumed to be _____.
10. $A \times B$; $A \cdot B$; $A(B)$ all mean A _____ B.
11. $I = P \times R \times T$ is an example of a _____.
12. $\frac{A}{B}$ means A _____ by B.
13. $1B$ is same as _____.
14. If the equation process is addition, solve for the unknown by _____.
15. You do not _____ or divide an equation by zero.
16. When solving for an unknown that involves more than one step, do _____ and _____ before multiplication and division.
17. If an equation contains parenthesis, first multiply _____ _____ inside the parenthesis by the number or letter outside the parenthesis.

7.	X
8.	fixed
9.	one
10.	times
11.	formula
12.	divided
13.	B
14.	subtraction
15.	multiply
16.	addition; subtraction
17.	each item

Calculations/Applications

Do calculations on scrap paper as needed. Worked-out solutions are provided at end.

18. $P - \$40 = \$70$. $P =$ _____.
19. $\frac{1}{7}V = 900$. $V =$ _____.
20. $5C - C = 100$. $C =$ _____.
       $5C =$ _____.
21. $5W + 2(10 - W) = 50$. $W =$ _____.
22. Situation 5 in LU 5–2 is when total units _____ _____ _____ and know which sells better.
23. Situation 6 in LU 5–2 is when total units _____ _____ and don't know which sells best.
24. A pair of Reebok sneakers was reduced $40. The sale price was $90. The original price was _____.
25. A local KFC restaurant budgets $\frac{1}{12}$ of its monthly profits on salaries. Salaries for the month were $6,000. The monthly profit for KFC was _____.
26. Lowell Co. sold 6 times as many lamps as Ryan Co. The difference in their sales is 125. Lowell sold _____ lamps.
27. Al and Pete sold 400 homes for Century 21 Real Estate. Al sold seven times as many homes as Pete. Al sold _____ homes.

18.	$110
19.	6,300
20.	$C = 25$ $5C = 125$
21.	$W = 10$
22.	are not given
23.	are given
24.	$130
25.	$72,000
26.	150
27.	350

28. On Monday, Smith Co. sold $350 worth of calculators ($12) and watches ($10). Customers bought 5 times as many calculators as watches. How many calculators and watches did Smith sell on Monday?

29. On Monday, Smith Co. sold calculators ($12) and watches ($10). A total of 30 sales of watches and calculators were $350. How many of each did Smith sell?

28.	25 calculators; 5 watches
29.	25 calculators; 5 watches

Worked-Out Solutions to Calculations/Applications Section

18.
$$P - \$40 = \$\ 70$$
$$\underline{+\ 40 = +\ 40}$$
$$P\qquad = \$110$$

19.
$$\frac{1}{7}V = \ 900$$
$$7\left(\frac{1}{7}V\right) = \ 900\,(7)$$
$$V = 6{,}300$$

20.
$$5C - C = 100$$
$$\frac{4C}{4} = \frac{100}{4}$$
$$C = 25$$
$$5C = 125$$

21.
$$5W + 20 - 2W = \ 50$$
$$3W + 20 = \ 50$$
$$\underline{-20 = -20}$$
$$\frac{3W}{3} = \frac{30}{3}$$
$$W = 10$$

24.
$$P - \$40 = \$\ 90$$
$$\underline{+\ 40\quad +\ 40}$$
$$P\qquad = \$130$$

25.
$$\frac{1}{12}P = \$6{,}000$$
$$12\left(\frac{1}{12}\right)P = \$6{,}000\,(12)$$
$$P = \$72{,}000$$

26.
$$6L - L = 125$$
$$\frac{5L}{5} = \frac{125}{5}$$
$$L = 25 \qquad 25 \times 6 = 150$$

27.
$$7H + H = 400$$
$$\frac{8H}{8} = \frac{400}{8}$$
$$H = 50 \qquad 7 \times 50 = 350$$

28.

Calculators	$5W$	12	$60W$
Watches	$W*$	10	$+\ 10W$
			$\$350$

$$60W + 10W = 350 \qquad \text{25 calculators}$$
$$\frac{70W}{70} = \frac{350}{70} \qquad \text{5 watches}$$
$$W = 5$$

For Situation 5, assign variable to one that sells the least.

29.

Calculators	$C*$	12	$12C$
Watches	$30 - C$	10	$+\ 10(30 - C)$
			$\$350$

$$12C + 10(30 - C) = \ 350$$
$$12C + 300 - 10C = \ 350$$
$$2C + 300 = \ 350$$
$$\underline{-\ 300 = -\ 300}$$
$$\frac{2C}{2} = \frac{50}{2} \qquad \text{25 calculators}$$
$$C = 25 \qquad \text{5 watches}$$
$$(30 - 25) = 5$$

For Situation 6, assign variable to most expensive.

Word Problem Practice Quiz

Check with your instructor for complete worked-out solutions.

5–1. What number decreased by 605 equals 1,090?

5–2. One eighth of all sales at Al's Diner are for cash. If cash sales for the week were $1,250, what were Al's total sales?

5–3. Christina is 9 times Judith's age. If the difference in their age is 24, how old is each?

5–4. D. Darby and J. Jonathan sell cars for Jean's Auto. Over the past year they sold 290 cars. Assume Darby sells 4 times as many cars as Jonathan. How many cars did each sell?

5–5. The Computer Store sells diskettes ($3) and boxes of computer paper ($4). If total sales were

$3,100 and customers bought 9 times as many diskettes as boxes of computer paper, what would be the number of each sold? Show proof that unit sales do equal the total dollar sales.

5–6. Pens cost $6 per carton, and rubber bands cost $4 per carton. If an order comes to a total of 70 cartons for $300, what was the specific number of cartons of pens as well as rubber bands? (Hint: Let *P* equal cartons of pens.)

5–7. Jim Murray and Phyllis Lowe received a total of $250,000 from a deceased relative's estate. They decided to put away $50,000 in a trust for their child and divide the remainder into $\frac{3}{4}$ for Phyllis and $\frac{1}{4}$ for Jim. How much will Phyllis and Jim receive?

5–8. In Ajax Corporation, the first shift produced $4\frac{1}{2}$ times as many lightbulbs as the second shift.

If the number of lightbulbs produced was 55,000, how many lightbulbs were produced on each shift?

5–9. Jarvis Company sells thermometers ($4) and hot water bottles ($9). If total sales were $825 and customers bought 6 times as many thermometers as hot water bottles, what would be the number of each sold? Check that your result is equal to total dollar sales.

5–10. Wrenches cost $120 per carton and hammers cost $400 per carton. An order comes in for a total of 70 cartons for $15,400. How many cartons of wrenches and hammers are involved? Check your answer. (Hint: Let *H* equal hammers.)

CHAPTER 6

Self-Paced Worksheet

Cover the answers on the right and fill in each blank. After answering the question, look to the right for your answer.

Vocabulary Review

1. The _____ is the beginning whole quantity to which something is being compared.
2. The _____ is a percent, decimal, or fraction that indicates the part of the base you must calculate.
3. The _____ stands for hundredths.
4. The _____ is the amount or part that results from multiplying the base times the rate.
5. The _____ _____ is the decrease in price divided by the original amount.
6. The _____ _____ is the increase in price divided by the original amount.

1. base
2. rate

3. percent
4. portion

5. percent decrease
6. percent increase

Theory Tips (and/or Cautions)

7. .008 means $\frac{8}{10}$ of _____ percent.
8. When a percent is less than 1%, the decimal conversion has at least _____ leading zeros before the whole number.
9. In rounding percents, digits to the right of the identified digit will be _____.
10. 22.5% is an example of a _____ percent.
11. In converting a mixed percent to a fraction first convert it to an _____ _____ before multiplying by 1/100.
12. The portion could be larger than the base if the rate is _____ than 100%.
13. The old year, or old price would be the _____.
14. In an increase or decrease problem, the difference in the price would be the _____.
15. The portion and rate will refer to the same part of the _____.
16. The base will be larger than the portion if the rate is _____ than 100%.
17. Portion = Base × _____.
18. The base represents _____ percent.
19. If sales are up to $4,000 a 20% increase in the new year and we are looking for sales in the old year the rate will be _____ percent of the old year.
20. The _____ is larger than the base if the rate is greater than 100%.

7. one
8. two

9. deleted
10. decimal
11. improper fraction

12. greater
13. base
14. portion
15. base
16. less
17. rate
18. 100
19. 120%

20 portion

Calculations/Applications

Do calculations on scrap paper as needed. Worked-out solutions are provided at end.

21. .006 converted to a percent is _____.
22. $7\frac{3}{4}$% converted to a decimal is _____.
23. $\frac{17}{22}$ converted to a percent is _____ (round to the nearest hundredth percent).
24. $14\frac{1}{4}$% converted to a fraction is _____.
25. 11.4% converted to a fraction is _____.
26. Twelve out of 29 students in Professor Okimato's class received an "A" grade. What percent of the class did not receive the "A" grade? (Round to the nearest tenth percent.)
27. Computer City has yet to receive 70% of his computer order. Computer City received 90 computers to date. What was the original order?
28. In 2005, a local Pizza Hut shop had sales of $450,000. In 2006, sales were up 30%. What are the shop sales in 2006?
29. The price of a Saab 9000 increased in price from $24,500 to $29,000. What was the percent increase? (Round to the nearest hundredth percent.)

21. .6%
22. .0775
23. 77.27%
24. $\frac{57}{400}$
25. $\frac{57}{500}$
26. 58.6%

27. 300 computers

28. $585,000

29. 18.37%

Worked-Out Solutions to Calculations/Applications Section

22. $7\% = .07$

$\dfrac{3}{4}\% = .0075$ $\Big\} = .0775$

23. $77.2727\% \to 77.27\%$
  ↑

24. $14\dfrac{1}{4}\% = \dfrac{57}{4} \times \dfrac{1}{100} = \dfrac{57}{400}$

25. $11.4\% \to 11\dfrac{4}{10}$

$\to \dfrac{114}{10} \times \dfrac{1}{100}$

$= \dfrac{114}{1,000}$

$= \dfrac{57}{500}$

26.	12 A's 29 students	Percent did not receive A	B: 29 R: ? P: 17 (29 − 12)	P 17 / B 29 × R ? $\dfrac{17}{29} = 58.62\%$ $= 58.6\%$
27.	70% of order not in 90 computers received	Original order	B: ? R: .30 (100% − 70%) P: 90	P 90 / B ? × R .30 $\dfrac{90}{.30} = 300$

Note: 90 computers is 30% of the total, not 70%.

28.	2005 $450,000 in sales 2006 Sales up 30%	Sales of 2006	B: $450,000 R: 1.30 (100% + 30%) P: ?	P ? / $450,000 1.30 / B × R $450,000 × 1.30 $585,000

Note: The Portion is larger than the Base since Rate is greater than 100%.

29.	$24,500 old price $29,000 new price	Percent increase	B: $24,500 (orig) R: ? P: $4,500 (diff. in price)	P $4,500 / B $24,500 × R ? $\dfrac{\$4,500}{\$24,500} = 18.367\% = 18.37\%$

Keep in mind:
a. The Portion and Rate must relate to same piece of the Base.
b. The Portion will be larger than the Base if the Rate is greater than 100%.

Word Problem Practice Quiz

Check with your instructor for complete worked-out solutions.

6–1. A stove increased in price from $650 to $1,280. What was the percent of increase? Round to the nearest hundredth percent.

6–2. The price of a calculator dropped from $38.95 to $17.49. What was the percent decrease in price? Round to nearest tenth percent.

6–3. Joan Smith bought an IBS Personal Computer priced at $1,688. She put down 40%. What is the amount of the down payment Joan made?

6–4. Earl Miller receives an annual salary of $50,000 from PB Stationery. Today his boss informs him that he will be getting a $4,700 raise. What percent of his old salary is the $4,700 raise? Round to nearest tenth percent.

6–5. Northwest Community College has 4,900 female students. This represents 70% of the total student body. How many students attend NW Community College?

6–6. At the Museum of Fine Arts it was estimated that 40% of all visitors are from in state. On Saturday, 7,000 people attended the museum. What is the number of out-of-state people in attendance?

6–7. Sharon Fox, insurance agent, earned a commission of $840 in her first week on the job. Her commission percent is 12%. What were Sharon's total sales for the week?

6–8. John's Bookstore ordered 500 business math texts. On verifying the order, only 80 books were actually received. What percent of the order was missing?

6–9. Joshua Wright was reviewing the total accounts receivable. This month he received $180,000 from credit customers. This represented 60% of all receivables due. What is the total amount of Joshua Wright's accounts receivable?

6–10. Veek Company in 2008 had sales of $950,000. In 2009, sales were up 66%. Calculate the sales for 2009.

CHAPTER 7

Self-Paced Worksheet

Cover the answers on the right and fill in each blank. After answering the question, look to the right for your answer.

Vocabulary Review

1. A _____ _____ is the result of making an early payment within the discount period.
2. _____ _____ is the list price less the amount of trade discount.
3. _____ _____ _____ rate is found by taking the complement of each term in the discount and multiplying them together. This rate shows the actual cost to the buyer for each dollar. This rate is not rounded.
4. 1 − Net price equivalent rate equals the _____ _____ _____ rate. This rate is not rounded.
5. A _____ _____ is two or more trade discounts that are applied to the balance remaining after the previous discount is taken.
6. The amount of time to take advantage of a cash discount is the _____ _____.
7. If the discount period is missed, payment is due by the end of the _____ _____.
8. _____ _____ means seller pays cost of freight to get goods to buyer's location.
9. _____ _____ _____ means buyer pays cost of freight to getting goods to his location.
10. _____ means the same as end of month.
11. The _____ _____ is the suggested retail price paid by customers.
12. The _____ is 100% less the stated percent.

1.	cash discount
2.	net price
3.	net price equivalent
4.	single equivalent discount
5.	chain discount
6.	discount period
7.	credit period
8.	FOB destination
9.	FOB shipping point
10.	proximo
11.	list price
12.	complement

Theory Tips (and/or Cautions)

13. Trade discounts may be _____ discounts or a _____ of discounts.
14. Trade discounts are not taken on _____, returned goods, or sales tax.
15. _____ _____ are never added together.
16. The _____ _____ _____ _____ is never rounded.
17. The _____ price times the net price equivalent rate is rounded to the nearest cent.
18. The _____ _____ _____ rate shows what the buyer saves per dollar.
19. _____ _____ should be taken before cash discounts.
20. Cash discounts are taken on the _____ _____.
21. FOB destination means the _____ pays the freight cost.
22. When using the exact days in a year calendar, if the two dates are in the same year you take the _____ between the table look-up number.
23. When using the exact days in a year calendar, if the two dates are in different years from the first year table look-up will have to be _____ from 365.
24. If credit terms are 2/10 EOM and purchase is on November 5, the _____ _____ ends on December 10.
25. If credit terms are 2/10 EOM and purchase is on April 29, the discount period ends on _____.
26. Partial payments are calculated by what you can afford. The partial payment is divided by one _____ the discount rate.

13.	single; chain
14.	freight
15.	chain discounts
16.	net price equivalent rate
17.	list
18.	single equivalent discount
19.	trade discounts
20.	net price
21.	seller
22.	difference
23.	subtracted
24.	discount period
25.	June 10
26.	minus

Calculations/Applications

Do calculations on scrap paper as needed. Worked-out solutions are provided at end.

27. A chain discount of 15/3/2 results in a net price equivalent rate of _____.

27.	.80801

77

28. The single equivalent discount rate in #27 would be _____.

29. A cellular phone had a list price of $250 with a chain discount of 8/6. Calculate the net price and trade discount amount.

30. Complete the following:

Invoice date	Date goods received	Terms	Last day of discount period	End of credit period
a. July 8		1/10,n/30	?	?
b. March 8		2/10 EOM	?	?
c. July 9	Oct. 4	3/10,n/30 ROG	?	?
d. March 26		2/10 EOM	?	?

31. Given the following, calculate cash discount and amount paid.

Gross amount of invoice including freight, $900
Freight, $100
Invoice date, 9/6
Terms, 1/10 EOM
Date of payment, 10/9

32. Calculate the amount to be credited and balance outstanding from the following partial payment information.

Invoice amount, $950
Terms, 2/10, n/60
Invoice date, 9/20
Partial payment date, 9/27
Partial payment, $400

33. A Goodyear Tire Shop received an invoice showing 5 tires at $40 each, 9 tires at $70 each and 20 tires at $90 each. Shipping terms are FOB shipping point. Freight is $200. Trade discount is 10/9 and a cash discount of 2/10, N/30 is offered. Assuming Goodyear pays within the discount period, what did Goodyear pay?

28. .19199
29. $216.20 net price; $ 33.80 trade discount
30. **a.** July 18 Aug. 7
b. Apr. 10 Apr. 30
c. Oct. 14 Nov. 3
d. May 10 May 30
31. $8.00 $892
32. $408.16 $541.84
33. $2,310.89

Worked-Out Solutions to Calculations/Applications Section

27.
$$
\begin{array}{ccc}
100\% & 100\% & 100\% \\
-\ 15\% & -\ 3\% & -\ 2\% \\
\hline
.85 \times & .97 \times & .98 = .80801
\end{array}
$$

28.
$$
\begin{array}{r}
1.00000 \\
-\ .80801 \\
\hline
.19199
\end{array}
$$

29.
$$
\begin{array}{ccc}
100\% & 100\% & 1.0000 \\
-\ 8\% & -\ 6\% & -\ .8648 \\
\hline
.92 \times & .94 = & .8648 \text{ NPER} \quad .1352 \text{ SEDR} \\
& & \times\ \$250 \quad\quad \times\ \$250 \\
& & \$216.20 \quad\quad \$33.80
\end{array}
$$

30. a. July 8   189
$$
\begin{array}{r}
+\ 30 \\
\hline
219 \rightarrow \text{Aug. 7}
\end{array}
$$
   c. Oct. 4   277
$$
\begin{array}{r}
+\ 30 \\
\hline
307 \rightarrow \text{Nov. 3}
\end{array}
$$

b. Cash discount ends after first 10 days of month that follows the sale. Credit period ends 20 days after discount period.

d. Cash discount ends after first 10 days of second month that follows the sale. Credit period ends 20 days after discount period.

31.
$$
\begin{array}{r}
\$900 \\
-\ 100 \\
\hline
\$800 \times .01 = \$8.00 \\
\$800 \times .99 = \$792 + \$100 = \$892
\end{array}
$$

32. $\dfrac{\$400}{1-.02} = \dfrac{\$400}{.98} = \$408.16$
$$
\begin{array}{r}
\$950.00 \\
-\ 408.16 \\
\hline
\$541.84
\end{array}
$$

33.

$5 \times \$40 = \$\ \ 200$
$9 \times \$70 = \ \ \ \ 630$
$20 \times \$90 = \underline{\ \ 1,800}$
$\$2,630$ total list

100%	100%
− 10%	− 9%

$.90 \ \times \ .91 \ = \ \ \ \ \ .819$
$\times \ \ \$2,630$
$\overline{\$2,153.97}$

$\$2,153.97 \times .98 = \$2,110.89$
$\underline{+\ \ 200.00}$
$\$2,310.89$

Word Problem Practice Quiz

Check with your instructor for complete worked-out solutions.

7-1. Alvin Corporation buys wood stoves from a wholesaler. The list price of a wood stove is $700, with a trade discount of 35%. Find the amount of trade discount and the net price of this stove.

7-2. Algene Bookstore paid a net price of $7,400 for the coming semester. The publisher offered a trade discount of 25%. What was the publisher's original list price?

7-3. Bob's Radio Shop wants to buy a line of new shortwave radios. Manufacturer A offers chain discounts of 19/10, while Manufacturer B offers terms of 18/11. Assume both manufacturers have the same list price. Which manufacturer should Bob buy from?

7-4. John's Dress Shop received an invoice dated November 8 for $1,619, with terms of 3/10, 2/15, n/60. On November 23, John's Dress Shop sent a partial payment of $715. What is the actual amount that should be credited? What is John's Dress Shop's outstanding balance?

7-5. An invoice dated 5/16/XX received by Jack's Supply indicated a balance of $7,200. This balance included a freight charge of $400. Terms of the bill were 3/10, 2/30, n/60. Assume Jack pays off the bill on May 25. What amount will he pay?

7-6. B Tool Manufacturer sold a set of jigsaws to Buy Hardware. The list price was $1,520. B Tool offered a chain discount of 4/3/2. What was the net price of the jigsaws, and what was the total of the trade discount? Round these two answers to nearest cent.

7-7. Smith of Boston sold office equipment for $12,500 to Frank of Los Angeles. Terms of the sale are 2/10, n/30 FOB Boston. Smith has agreed to prepay the freight of $120. Assume Frank pays within the discount period. How much will they pay Smith?

7-8. A manufacturer of ice skates offered chain discounts of 6/5/1 to many of its customers. Bob's Sporting Goods ordered 30 pairs of ice skates that had a total list price of $1,800. What was the net price paid by Bob's Sporting Goods? What was the amount of the trade discount? Round answers to nearest cent.

7-9. A living room set lists for $9,000 and carries a trade discount of 30%. Freight (FOB shipping point) of $70 is not part of list price. Calculate the net price (also include cost of freight) of the living room set assuming a cash discount of 4%. What was amount of trade discount?

7-10. An invoice dated February 9 in the amount of $45,000 is received by Reliance Corporation on February 13. Cash discount terms on the invoice are 2/10, n/30. On February 18, Reliance mails a check in the amount of $9,000 as partial payment on the invoice. What is the amount of discount Reliance should receive?

CHAPTER 8

Self-Paced Worksheet
(Items with an asterisk (*) are not covered in the

Cover the answers on the right and fill in each blank. After answering the question, look to t

Vocabulary Review

1. The _____ _____ is the selling price less cost.
2. Gross profit minus operating expenses equals net _____.
3. The _____ is the price paid to supplier to bring merchandise into the store.
4. The original selling price less the reduction to sale price equals the _____ _____.
5. Net sales minus costs equals _____ _____.
6. Cost plus markup equals _____ _____.
7. The regular expenses of doing business are called _____ expenses.
8. Dollar markup divided by cost equals _____ _____ on _____.
9. Dollar markup divided by selling price equals _____ _____ on _____.
10. The dollar markdown divided by the original selling price equals _____ _____.

1. dollar markup
2. income
3. cost
4. dollar markdown
5. gross profit
6. selling price
7. operating
8. percent markup; cost
9. percent markup; selling price
10. markdown percent

Theory Tips (and/or Cautions)

11. When markup is based on cost the cost is assumed to be _____ percent.
12. Selling price equals _____ plus markup.
13. The dollar markup divided by percent markup on cost equals the _____.
14. When markup is based on cost, the cost is the _____.
15. When markup is based on cost, the portion is the _____ _____.
16. When markup is based on selling price, the selling price is assumed to be _____ percent.
17. The dollar markup divided by percent markup on selling price equals the _____ _____.
18. When markup is based on selling price, the selling price is the _____.
19. When markup is based on selling price, the portion is the _____.
20. In markdowns, the dollar markdown is the _____.
21. The _____ _____ _____ in a markdown is considered to be the base.

22.* For perishables, markup is based on _____.
23. Break even point is _____ _____ divided by contribution margin.

11. 100
12. cost
13. cost
14. base
15. selling price
16. 100
17. selling price
18. base
19. cost
20. portion
21. original selling price
22. $404.44
23. Fixed cost

Calculations/Applications
Do calculations on scrap paper as needed. Worked-out solutions are provided at end.

24. Neal Wall bought a computer from A.C. Suppliers for $1,200. Neal plans to resell the computer for $1,800. What is Neal Wall's dollar markup and his percent markup on cost? Check your answer.

24. $600 markup; 50% markup on cost

25. Fred Miguel bought rings for his jewelry shop that cost $90 each. Fred must mark up each ring 40% on cost. What is the dollar markup? What is the selling price of each ring? Check your answer.

25. $36; $126

26. Alice Rone sells watches. Her competitor sells a new line of watches for $30 each. Alice needs a 30% markup on cost to make her desired profit, and she must meet price competition. What cost can Alice afford to bring these watches into the store? What is the dollar markup?

26. $23.08; $6.92

27. Neal Wall bought a computer from A.C. Suppliers for $1,200. Neal plans to resell the computer for $1,800. What is Neal Wall's dollar markup and his percent markup on selling price? (Round to the nearest tenth percent.)

27. $600; 33.3%

28. Fred Miguel bought rings for his jewelry shop that cost $90 each. Fred must mark up each ring 40% on selling price. What is the selling price of each ring? What is the dollar markup? Check your answer.

28. $150; $60

29. Alice Rone sells watches. Her competitor sells a new line of watches for $30 each. Alice needs a 30% markup on selling price to make her desired profit, and she must meet price competition. What cost can Alice afford to bring these watches into the store? What is the dollar markup?

29. $21; $9

30. Pete Burrows sells hammers for $14 that cost $8. What is Pete's percent markup at cost? (Round to the nearest tenth percent.) What is Pete's percent markup on selling price? (Round to the nearest hundredth percent.)

30. 75% on cost; 42.86% on selling price

31. Staples bought an office desk for $400 and marked it up 30% on selling price to promote customer interest. Staples marked the desk down 5% for one week. After a week, Staples marked the desk up 2%. The last week it marked it down 8%. What is the final selling price?

31. $509.41

32. Joe Kiim owns a bakery. Joe baked 40 dozen bagels. Joe expects a 20% spoilage rate. The bagels cost $1.10 per dozen. Joe wants a 70% markup on cost. What should Joe charge for each dozen bagels? (Round to the nearest cent.)

32. $2.34 per dozen

33. Jane corporation produces Sweatshirts for a selling price of $19.25. Their variable cost is $13.10. Assuming a fixed cost of $6,150 what is Jane corporation's break even point?

33. 1,000 Sweatshirts

Worked-Out Solutions to Calculations/Applications Section

24. $1,800 - $1,200 = $600 $\dfrac{\$600}{\$1,200} = 50\%$

Check: $\dfrac{\$600}{.50} = \$1,200$

25. $S = C + M$
$S = \$90 + .40(\$90)$
$S = \$90 + \$36$ or   Check: $1.40 \times \$90 = \$126$
$S = \$126$

26.* $S = C + M$
$\$30 = C + .30C$
$\dfrac{\$30}{1.30} = \dfrac{\cancel{1.30}C}{\cancel{1.30}}$ or $\dfrac{\$30}{1 + .30} = \dfrac{\$30}{1.30} = \$23.08$
$\$23.08 = C$
$\$30 - \$23.08 = \$6.92$ markup

27. $S = C + M$
$\$1,800 = \$1,200 + M$
$\$600 = M$
$\dfrac{\$600}{\$1,800} = 33.3\%$

28.* $S = C + M$
$S = \$90 + .40S$
$\dfrac{-.40S \qquad -.40S}{\dfrac{\cancel{.60}S}{\cancel{.60}} = \dfrac{\$90}{.60}}$ or $\dfrac{\$90}{1 - .40} = \dfrac{\$90}{.60} = \$150$
$S = \$150$
$\$150 - \$90 = \$60$ markup

29.* $S = C + M$
$\$30 = C + .30(\$30)$
$\$30 = C + \$9$ or $C = \$30(1 - .30)$
$\dfrac{-9 \qquad\quad -9}{\$21 = C}$ $C = \$30(.70)$
$\$30 - \$21 = \$9$ markup $C = \$21$

81

30.

$$\begin{array}{r} \$14 \\ -\ 8 \\ \hline \$\ 6 \end{array} \qquad \frac{\$6}{\$8} = 75\% \qquad \frac{\$6}{\$14} = 42.86\%$$

31.*
$$S = C + M$$
$$S = \$400 + .30S$$
$$\begin{array}{cc} -.30S & -\ .30S \\ \hline \dfrac{.70S}{.70} = \dfrac{\$400}{.70} \end{array} \qquad \text{or} \qquad \dfrac{\$400}{1 - .30} = \dfrac{\$400}{.70} = \$571.43$$
$$S = \$571.43$$
$$\$571.43 \times\ .95 = \$542.86$$
$$\$542.86 \times 1.02 = \$553.71$$
$$\$553.71 \times\ .92 = \$509.41$$

32.
$$TS = TC + TM$$
$$TS = \$44 + .70(\$44) \qquad \$1.10 \times 40 = \$44\ TC$$
$$TS = \$74.80$$
$$\dfrac{\$74.80}{32} = \$2.34 \text{ per dozen}$$

33.
$$\dfrac{6,150}{(\$19.25 - \$13.10)} = 1,000$$

Word Problem Practice Quiz

Check with your instructor for complete worked-out solutions.

8–1. A computer sells for $820 and is marked up 40% of the selling price. What is the cost of the computer?

8–2. Bob Hoffman sells a radio for $189.19 that cost him $91.50. What was Bob's percent of markup based on the selling price? Round to nearest percent. Check your answer. Will be slightly off due to rounding.

8–3. Reese Company buys a watch at a cost of $48.50. Reese plans to sell the watch for $79.99. What is the dollar markup as well as percent markup on cost? Round to nearest hundredth percent. Check your answer. Will be slightly off due to rounding.

8–4. Bill Spread, owner of the Bedding Shop, knows that his customers will pay no more than $300 for a comforter. Assume Bill wants a 30% markup on selling price. What is the most he could pay the manufacturer for this comforter?

8–5. John Mills sells ski gloves. He knows the most that people will pay for the gloves is $39.99. John is convinced that he needs a 28% markup based on cost. What is the most that John can pay to his supplier for gloves and still keep his selling price constant? Round to nearest cent.

8–6. Al's Department Store bought a sterling silver set for $518. Jim wants to mark up the set at 48% of the selling price. What should be the selling price of the sterling set? Round to nearest cent.

8–7. At the end of the summer, lawn mowers were advertised for 35% off regular price. John Mills saw a lawn mower with a regular price of $199. What is the dollar markdown as well as the sale price?

8–8. Mr. Fry, store manager for Vic's Appliance, is having a difficult time placing a selling price on a refrigerator that cost $899. Mr. Fry knows his boss would like to have a 35% markup based on cost. Could you help Mr. Fry with the calculation?

8–9. Angie's Bake Shop makes decorated chocolate chip cookies that cost $.30 each. Past experience shows that 20% of the cookies will crack and have to be discarded. Assume Angie wants a 65% markup based on cost and produces 400 cookies. What price should each cookie sell for? Round to nearest cent.

8–10. Lee company produces drills with a selling price of $49.99. It's varible cost's is $31.55. Assuming a fixed cost of $276,600 what is Lee company's break even point?

CHAPTER 9

Self-Paced Worksheet

Cover the answers on the right and fill in each blank. After answering the question, look to the right for your answer.

Vocabulary Review

1. _____ means being paid 26 times in a year.
2. The ____ ____ ____ ____ sets minimum wage standards and overtime regulations.
3. _____ _____ represents earnings before deductions.
4. A _____ _____ schedule is based on different levels of production.
5. A _____ represents an advance that will have to be repaid.
6. A _____ _____ scale uses different commission rates for different levels of net sales.
7. FICA tax requires separate reporting for _____ _____ and _____.
8. The _____ _____ method or the _____ method may be used to calculate amount of federal income tax withheld.
9. _____ _____ _____ may vary from state to state.
10. A _____ _____ is a multicolumn form to record payroll.

1.	biweekly
2.	Fair Labor Standards Act
3.	gross pay
4.	differential pay
5.	draw
6.	variable commission
7.	Social Security; Medicare
8.	wage bracket; percentage
9.	State unemployment tax
10.	payroll register

Theory Tips (and/or Cautions)

11. A _____ is made up of thirteen weeks.
12. Biweekly period is 26 times per year, while _____ is 24 times.
13. If an overtime rate is grater than two decimal places _____ _____ round it.
14. Net pay plus _____ equals gross pay.
15. A draw is an _____ on a salesperson's commission.
16. The taxable earnings column of a _____ _____ shows the wages subject to the tax, not the actual deduction.
17. _____ has no base cut off while Social Security does.
18. The _____ _____ is used by companies that do not want to store wage bracket tables.
19. The _____ pays for state and federal unemployment.

11.	quarter
12.	semimonthly
13	do not
14.	deductions
15.	advance
16.	payroll register
17.	Medicare
18.	employer

Calculations/Applications

Do calculations on scrap paper as needed. Worked-out solutions are provided at end.

19. Calculate the total gross pay for Melvin Moore. Assume time and half for overtime. Melvin earns $8 per hour.

    Melvin's hours worked

M	T	W	Th	F	Sat
5	12	8	7	9	14

20. Based on the following schedule, what is Ron's gross pay? Ron had net sales of $180,000.

Up to $40,000	6%
$40,000–$60,000	7%
Over $60,000	$7\frac{1}{2}$%

21. Assume a 6.20% Social Security rate on $97,500 and a Medicare rate of 1.45%. What will Alice pay in, for Social Security and Medicare for this week's payroll of $1,500? To date, her cumulative earnings before this payroll were $96,300.

19.	$500
20.	$12,800
21.	SS $74.40; Med $21.75

22. From the following information, calculate Pat's net pay. Use the wage bracket table for FIT.

Employee	Status	Claims	Gross pay	FIT	FICA SS/Med	Net pay
Pat Swan	M	2	$930			

23. Lloyd Alex has two employees who earn $500 and $800 a week. Assume a 5.4% FUTA rate. What will Lloyd pay for SUTA and FUTA for the first quarter?

Worked-Out Solutions to Calculations/Applications Section

19. Total hours = 55
40 hours × $8 = $320
15 hours × $12 = $180
$500

20. ($40,000 × .06) + ($20,000 × .07) + ($120,000 × .075)
$2,400 + $1,400 + $9,000 = $12,800

21. Social Security   Medicare

$97,500 $1,500 × .0145 = $21.75
− 96,300
$ 1,200 × .062 = $74.40

22. FIT: $930.00
− 130.76 ($65.38 × 2)
$799.24
− 449.00
$350.24 = ($29.50 + .15 (350.24))
$29.50 $52.54   = $82.04 FIT

SS: $930 × .062 = $57.66
Med: $930 × .062 = $13.49
Net pay: $930 − $82.04 − $57.66 − $13.49 = $776.81

23.   Exempt wages
13 weeks × $500 = $ 6,500   −0−
13 weeks × $800 = $10,400 $3,400
$16,900

$16,900 − $3,400 = $13,500 taxable wages

SUTA: .054 × $13,500 = $729
FUTA: .008 × $13,500 = $108

Word Problem Practice Quiz

Check with your instructor for complete worked-out solutions.

9–1. Read Jones is a salesclerk at Moe's Department Store. She is paid $7.50 per hour plus a commission of 3% on all sales. Assume Read works 35 hours and has sales of $4,800. What is her gross pay?

9–2. Staple Corporation pays its employees on a graduated commission scale: 5% on the first $40,000 sales; 6% on sales above $40,000 to $85,000; and 7% on sales greater than $85,000. Bill Burns had sales of $92,000. What commission did Bill earn?

9–3. John Hall earned $1,060 last week. He is married, paid biweekly, and claims two exemptions, What is his income tax? Use the percentage method.

9–4. Larry Johnson earns a gross salary of $3,000 each week. In week 30 what will Larry pay for Social Security and Medicare taxes?

9–5. Robyn Hartman earns $700 per week plus 5% of sales in excess of $7,000. If Robyn sells $20,000 the first week, how much are her earnings?

9–6. Joe Ross is an automobile salesman who receives a salary of $400 per week plus a commission of 6% on all sales. During a 4-week period he sold $46,900 worth of cars. What were Joe's average earnings?

9–7. B. Smith is a manager for Alve Corp. His earnings are subject to deductions for Social Security, Medicare, and FIT. B. Smith is $950 below the maximum for Social Security. What will his net pay for the week be if he earns $1,200? B. Smith is married, paid weekly, and claims three exemptions. Assume Social Security rate is 6.2% on $97,120 and Medicare is 1.45%. Use the wage bracket table for FIT.

9–8. Al Write is a salesman who receives a $1,600 draw per week. He receives a 12% commission on all sales. Sales for Al were $192,000 for the month. What did Al receive after taking the draw into consideration? Assume a 5-week month.

9–9. Angel Frank has a cumulative earnings of $97,400 at the end of June. The first week in July she earns $1,100. What is the total amount deducted for Social Security and Medicare?

9–10. Pete Lowe, who is single and paid monthly, earns $3,300 per month. He claims a withholding allowance of one. How much FIT is deducted from his paycheck using the percentage method?

CHAPTER 10

Self-Paced Worksheet

Cover the answers on the right and fill in each blank. After answering the question, look to the right for your answer.

Vocabulary Review

1. The ordinary interest method is known as the _____ _____.
2. _____ _____ equals principal plus interest.
3. _____ _____ represents the cost of a loan.
4. The _____ _____ method is used by the Federal Reserve banks and the federal government.
5. _____ interest uses 360 days.
6. The _____ is the amount of money that is originally borrowed, loaned, or deposited.
7. The U.S. _____ allows the borrower to receive proper interest credits when paying off a loan in more than one payment before the maturity date.
8. The _____ _____ _____ is principal times rate times time.

9. _____ can be expressed as years or fractional years, used to calculate the simple interest.
10. The _____ _____ results when a partial payment is subtracted from the principal in the U.S. Rule.

1. Banker's Rule
2. maturity value
3. simple interest
4. exact interest

5. ordinary
6. principal

7. Rule

8. simple interest formula

9. time

10. adjusted balance

Theory Tips (and/or Cautions)

11. _____ time periods can be days, months, or years.
12. Exact time can be found by the table in the *Business Math Handbook,* while _____ _____ represents 365 days.
13. Ordinary interest results in _____ interest than the exact time exact interest method.
14. _____ _____ are questioning the use of 360 days by banks.
15. In solving for the principal, given the interest, rate, and time the denominator will _____ _____ rounded.
16. When finding the time it can be converted to _____ by multiplying it by 360 or 365.
17. In the U.S. Rule, any partial payment is applied to cover the _____ due before the remainder of payment is used to lower the principal.
18. The last step of the U.S. Rule at maturity is to calculate interest from the last partial payment and _____ this interest to the adjusted balance.
19. In the U.S. Rule, the numerator of the interest calculation represents the _____ _____ _____ from previous payment date and goes to new payment date.

11. loan
12. exact interest

13. higher

14. consumer groups

15. not be

16. days

17. interest

18. add

19. number of days

Calculations/Applications

Do calculations on scrap paper as needed. Worked-out solutions are provided at end.

20. Simple interest on $15,000 at $4\frac{1}{2}$% for 8 months is _____.
21. Simple interest on $20,000 at $7\frac{1}{2}$% for 17 months is _____.
22. On June 8, Reed Ching borrowed $18,000 at 7%. Reed must pay the principal and interest on September 4. Using the exact interest method, the maturity value is _____.
23. The maturity value in #22 would be _____ using the ordinary interest method.

20. $450
21. $2,125
22. $18,303.78

23. $18,308

24. Complete the following (assume 360 days).

	Principal	Rate	Time	Simple interest
a.	?	6%	90 days	$18,000
b.	$6,000	?	300 days	$400
c.	$2,500	$7\frac{1}{2}$%	?	$550

25. Aray Foger borrowed $7,000 for 60 days at 7%. On day 20, Aray made a $800 partial payment. On day 45, Aray made a $1,200 partial payment. What is Aray's ending balance under the U.S. Rule?

Worked-Out Solutions to Calculations/Applications Section

20. $15,000 \times .045 \times \frac{8}{12} = $450

21. $20,000 \times .075 \times \frac{17}{12} = $2,125

22. Sept 4 → 247
June 8 → $\underline{159}$
   88    $18,000 \times .07 \times \frac{88}{365} = $303.78

$MV = $18,000 + $303.78 = $18,303.78

23. $18,000 \times .07 \times \frac{88}{360} = $308

$MV = $18,000 + $308 = $18,308

24. a. $\dfrac{$18,000}{.06 \times \frac{90}{360}} = $1,200,000$

b. $\dfrac{$400}{$6,000 \times \frac{300}{360}} = .08 = 8\%$

c. $\dfrac{$550}{$2,500 \times .075} = 2.9\overline{3} \times 360 = 1,056$ days

25. $7,000 \times .07 \times \frac{20}{360} = $27.22

$$\begin{array}{r} $800.00 \\ -\ 27.22 \\ \hline $772.78 \end{array}$$

$$\begin{array}{r} $7,000.00 \\ -\ 772.78 \\ \hline $6,227.22 \end{array} \times .07 \times \frac{25}{360} = $30.27$$

$$\begin{array}{r} $1,200.00 \\ -\ 30.27 \\ \hline $1,169.73 \end{array}$$

$$\begin{array}{r} $6,227.22 \\ -1,169.73 \\ \hline $5,057.49 \end{array} \times .07 \times \frac{15}{360} = $14.75$$

Balance owed $5,072.24 ($14.75 + $5,057.49)

Word Problem Practice Quiz

Check with your instructor for complete worked-out solutions.

10–1. Abby Ellen took out a loan of $45,000 to pay for her child's education. The loan would be repaid at the end of 8 years in one payment with $12\frac{1}{2}$% interest. How much interest is due? What is the total amount Abby has to pay at the end of the loan?

10–2. Jill Ring took out a simple interest loan for $20,000 at $6\frac{1}{2}$% for 19 months. What is the total interest cost (to nearest cent) for Jill?

10–3. Jennifer Rick went to Sunshine Bank to borrow $3,500 at a rate of $10\frac{3}{4}$%. The date of the loan was September 7. Jennifer hoped to repay the loan on January 15. Assume the loan is ordinary interest. What will be the interest cost on January 15? How much will Jennifer totally repay?

10–4. Jill Blum has a talk with Jennifer Rick (Problem 10–3) and suggests she consider the loan on exact interest. Recalculate the loan for Jennifer under this assumption.

10–5. Bob Lopes visited his local bank to see how long it will take for $1,000 to amount to $1,900 at a simple interest rate of 10%. Can you solve Bob's problem?

10–6. Margie Jones owns her own car. Her November monthly interest was $205. The rate is $13\frac{1}{2}$%. Find out what Margie's principal balance is at the beginning of November. Use 360 days. (In calculation, do not round denominator answer before dividing into numerator.)

10–7. Jane took out a loan for $16,800 at $9\frac{3}{4}$% on April 2, 2005. The loan is due January 8, 2006. Using exact time, ordinary interest, what is the interest cost? What total amount will Jane pay on January 8, 2006?

10–8. Terry Ball took out the same loan as Jane (Problem 10–7), but his terms were exact interest. What is Terry's difference in interest? What will Terry pay on January 8, 2006?

10–9. Bill Brody borrowed $12,500 on an 11% 120-day note. After 65 days, Bill paid $500 toward the note. On day 89, Bill paid an additional $4,500. What is the final balance due? Work out the total interest and ending balance due by the U.S. Rule.

CHAPTER 11

Self-Paced Worksheet

Cover the answers on the right and fill in each blank. After answering the question, look to the right for your answer.

Vocabulary Review

1. For a simple discount note the interest banks deduct in advance is the _____ _____ .
2. Principal plus interest equals _____ _____ .
3. The _____ _____ is also the principal of the note.
4. The company extending credit of an interest-bearing note is called the _____ .
5. The company issuing the note and borrowing the money is called the _____ .
6. A _____ note states that the borrower will repay a certain sum at a fixed time in the future.
7. The _____ of the note represents what one receives after deducting the bank discount from the maturity value of a note.
8. The _____ _____ is the true rate of interest.
9. A _____ _____ represents a loan to the federal government.
10. A _____ _____ _____ provides immediate financing up to an approved limit.

1. bank discount

2. maturity value
3. face value
4. payee
5. maker
6. promissory

7. proceeds

8. effective rate
9. Treasury bill
10. line of credit

Theory Tips (and/or Cautions)

11. The _____ _____ of the a non-interest-bearing note is the same as its face value.
12. A promissory note for a loan is usually _____ than one year.
13. The _____ _____ is higher for a simple discount note, since interest is deducted in advance.
14. The purchase price (or proceeds) of a Treasury bill is the value of the Treasury bill _____ the discount.
15. In the discounting process, the discount period represents the number of days the _____ will have to wait for the note to come due.
16. Instead of discounting notes, many companies set up _____ _____ _____ so that additional financing is immediately available.
17. A _____ _____ can be interest-bearing or noninterest-bearing.
18. In discounting an interest-bearing note before maturity, the first step is to calculate the _____ _____ .
19. To calculate the _____ _____ you must use the maturity value times the bank discount rate times the number of days the bank waits for the note to come due divided by 360.

11. maturity value
12. less
13. effective rate

14. less

15. bank

16. lines of credit

17. promissory note
18. maturity value

19. bank discount

Calculations/Applications

Do calculations on scrap paper as needed. Worked-out solutions are provided at end.

20. Andre Fox borrowed $15,000 on a noninterest-bearing, simple discount, $7\frac{1}{2}$%, 90-day note. Assume ordinary interest. What is (a) maturity value, (b) the bank's discount, (c) Andre's proceeds, and (d) the effective rate to nearest hundredth percent?

21. Joy Lindman buys a $10,000 13-week Treasury bill at $8\frac{1}{4}$%. What is her effective rate? Round to the nearest hundredth percent.

22. Frost Corporation accepted a $20,000, 8%, 90-day note on July 8. Frost discounts the note on September 6 at East Bank at 9%. What proceeds did Frost receive?

20. **a.** $15,000;
    b. $281.25;
    c. $14,718.75;
    d. 7.64%;

21. 8.42%

22. $20,247

Worked-Out Solutions to Calculations/Applications Section

20. **b.** $\$15,000 \times .075 \times \dfrac{90}{360} = \$281.25$

    c. $\$15,000 - \$281.25 = \$14,718.75$

    d. $\dfrac{\$281.25}{\$14,718.75 \times \dfrac{90}{360}} = 7.64\%$

21. $\$10,000 \times .0825 \times \dfrac{13}{52} = \$206.25$

    $\$10,000 - \$206.25 = \$9,793.75$

    $\dfrac{\$206.25}{\$9,793.75 \times \dfrac{13}{52}} = 8.42\%$

22. Interest $= \$20,000 \times .08 \times \dfrac{90}{360} = \$400$

    1. $MV = \$20,000 + \$400 = \$20,400$

    2. Sept. 6 → 249

        July 8 → 189

              60   90 − 60 = 30 days

    3. Bank discount $= \$20,400 \times .09 \times \dfrac{30}{360} = \$153$

    4. Proceeds $= \$20,400 - \$153 = \$20,247$

Word Problem Practice Quiz

Check with your instructor for complete worked-out solutions.

Use ordinary interest in your calculations.

11–1. James Bank discounts an 89-day note for $15,000 at 12%. Find the bank discount and proceeds.

11–2. In Problem 11–1, what is the effective rate of interest when the bank discounts the note at 12%? Round to nearest hundredth percent.

11–3. Jarvis Corporation accepted an $18,000 note on August 12. Terms of the note were $12\frac{3}{4}\%$ for 90 days. Jarvis discounted the note on September 20 at Shaw Bank at 13%. What net proceeds did Jarvis receive?

11–4. Michele Fross borrowed $6,000 for 120 days from Jones Bank. The bank discounted the note at 9%. What proceeds does Michele receive? Calculate effective interest rate to nearest hundredth percent.

11–5. On November 30, Smith Company accepted a 120-day, $15,000 noninterest-bearing note from B Manufacturer. What is the maturity value of the note?

11–6. On July 12 at the Sunshine Bank, Joyce Corporation discounted a $5,000, 90-day note dated June 20. Sunshine's discount rate was $11\frac{3}{4}\%$. How much did Joyce Corporation receive? Assume $5,000 is the maturity value.

11–7. Roger Corporation accepted an $8,000, 11%, 120-day note dated August 8 from June Company in settlement of a past bill. On October 25, Roger Corporation discounted the note at the bank at 12%. What is the note's maturity value, discount period, and bank discount? What are the net proceeds to Roger Corporation?

11–8. On April 12, Dr. Brown accepted a $10,000, 10%, 60-day note from Bill Moss granting a time extension on a past-due account. Dr. Brown discounted the note at the bank at 12% on May 20. What proceeds does Dr. Brown receive?

11–9. On May 5, Scott Rinse accepted a $12,000 note in granting a time extension of a bill for goods bought by Ron Prentice. Terms of the note were 13% for 90 days. On July 2, Scott could no longer wait for the money and discounted the note at Able Bank at 11%. What are Scott's proceeds?

11–10. Jensen Furniture wants to buy a $5,000 computer with a huge $1,000 cash discount. Jensen needs more cash to pay the bill. It is considering discounting a 120-day note dated May 12 with a maturity value of $5,000. Hunt Bank has a discount rate of 15% on May 18. Should Jensen discount the note?

CHAPTER 12

Self-Paced Worksheet

Cover the answers on the right and fill in each blank. After answering the question, look to the right for your answer.

Vocabulary Review

1. _____ is calculating the interest periodically over the life of the loan and adding it to the principal.
2. _____ _____ looks at how much money will have to be deposited today (or at some date) to reach a specific amount at maturity (in the future).
3. _____ are calculated by the number of years times the number of times compounded per year.
4. The _____ can be found by the annual rate divided by the number of times compounded per year.
5. Compounded _____ means the interest is calculated on the balance every six months.
6. The _____ _____ (APY) is calculated by the interest for 1 year divided by the principal.
7. The stated or _____ rate is one which the bank calculates interest.

Theory Tips (and/or Cautions)

8. To see how long to double a sum of money at different interest rates with annual compounding, divide 72 by the _____ _____.
9. Compounding goes from the present value to the _____ _____.
10. Present value goes from the future value to the _____ _____.
11. Compounded _____ means interest is calculated on the balance every 3 months.
12. Compound amounts less the principal equals _____ _____.
13. Compounding results in _____ interest than simple interest.
14. In the calculation of effective rate, the portion is the _____ for one year.
15. The APY or effective rate for $1 can be seen in the _____ table.
16. The table factors in the _____ _____ table are larger than 1.
17. The table factors in the _____ _____ table are less than 1.
18. A present value answer can be checked by using the _____ _____ table.

1.	compounding
2.	present value
3.	periods
4.	rate
5.	semiannually
6.	effective rate
7.	nominal
8.	interest rate
9.	future value
10.	present value
11.	quarterly
12.	compound interest
13.	higher
14.	interest
15.	compound
16.	compound interest
17.	present value
18.	compound value

Calculations/Applications

Do calculations on scrap paper as needed. Worked-out solutions are provided at end.

19. Alfred Rodriguez deposits $8,000 in Yoma Bank which pays 6% interest compounded quarterly. How much will Alfred have in his account at the end of 6 years?
20. Give the following, calculate the effective rate (to the nearest hundredth percent): Principal, $9,000; Interest rate, 8% compounded semiannually.
21. $1,800 compounded daily for 10 years will grow to _____ at 6.50%.
22. Jim Henson wants to buy his son a Toyota Land Cruiser in 5 years. The cost of the car should be $40,000. Assuming a bank rate of 6% compounded quarterly, how much must Jim put in the bank today?
23. Check your answer in #22 by the compound table.

19.	$11,436
20.	8.16%
21.	$3,447.72
22.	$29,700
23.	$40,002

Worked-Out Solutions to Calculations/Applications Section

19. $\frac{6\%}{4} = 1.5\%$ 6 yrs. × 4 = 24 periods

$8,000 × 1.4295 = $11,436

20. 4%, 2 periods (2 × 1)

$9,000 × 1.0816 = $9,734.40
    − 9,000.00
     $ 734.40

$\frac{\$734.40}{\$9,000} = 8.16\%$

21. $1,800 \times 1.9154 = $3,447.72

22. $\dfrac{6\%}{4} = 1\dfrac{1}{2}\%$ 5 yrs. $\times$ 4 = 20 periods

$40,000 \times .7425 = $29,700

23. $1\dfrac{1}{2}\%$, 20 periods   1.3469

$29,700 \times 1.3469 = $40,002   off slightly due to rounding of table factors.

Word Problem Practice Quiz

Check with your instructor for complete worked-out solutions.

12–1. Al Baker deposited $30,000 into Victory Bank which pays 12% interest compounded semiannually. How much will Al have in his account at the end of 4 years?

12–2. Ann Kate, owner of Ann's Sport Shop, loaned $13,000 to Rusty Katz to help him open an art shop. Rusty pans to repay Ann at the end of 5 years with 6% interest compounded quarterly. How much will Ann receive at the end of 5 years?

12–3. Jill Fonda opened a new savings account. She deposited $18,000 at 12% interest compounded semiannually. At the beginning of the year 4, Jill deposits an additional $50,000 that is also compounded semiannually at 12%. At the end of 6 years, what is the balance in Jill's account?

12–4. Rochelle Kotter wants to attend S.M.V. University. She will need $55,000 4 years from today. Her bank pays 12% interest compounded semiannually. What amount must Rochelle deposit today so she will have $55,000 in 4 years?

12–5. Margaret Foster wants to buy a new camper in 7 years. Margaret estimates the cost of the camper will be $7,200. If she invests $4,000 now, at a rate of 12% interest compounded semiannually, will she have enough money to buy her camper at the end of 7 years?

12–6. Karen is having difficulty deciding whether to put her savings in Mystic Bank or in Four Rivers Bank. Mystic offers a 10% interest rate compounded semiannually, while Four Rivers offers 12% interest compounded annually. Karen has $30,000 to deposit and expects to withdraw the money at the end of 5 years. Which bank gives Karen the best deal?

12–7. Steven deposited $15,000 at York Bank at 10% interest compounded semiannually. What was the effective rate? Round to nearest hundredth percent.

12–8. Al Miller, owner of Al's Garage, estimates that he will need $25,000 for new equipment in 20 years. Al decided to put aside the money today so it will be available in 20 years. His bank offers him 8% interest compounded semiannually. How much must Al invest today to have $25,000 in 20 years?

12–9. Ray Long wants to retire in Arizona when he is 70 years of age. He is now 55 and believes he will need $200,000 to retire comfortably. To date, Ray has set aside no retirement money. Assume Ray gets 12% interest compounded semiannually. How much must be invest today to meet his goal of $200,000?

12–10. Kevin Moore deposited $12,000 in a new savings account at 6% interest compounded quarterly. At the beginning of year 4, Kevin deposits an additional $40,000 also compounded quarterly at 6%. At the end of 6 years, what is the balance in Kevin's account?

CHAPTER 13

Self-Paced Worksheet

Cover the answers on the right and fill in each blank. After answering the question, look to the right for the answer.

Vocabulary Review

1. An _____ is a stream of equal payments made at periodic times.
2. An _____ _____ is an annuity that is paid (or received) at the end of the time period.
3. An _____ _____ is an annuity that is paid (or received) at the beginning of the time period.
4. Annuities that have stated beginning and ending dates are called _____ _____.
5. Beginning and ending dates of _____ _____ are uncertain (not fixed).
6. A _____ _____ is an annuity in which the stream of deposits with appropriate interest will equal a specified amount in the future.
7. The _____ _____ _____ _____ is the amount of money needed today to receive a specified steam (annuity) of money in the future.

1.	annuity
2.	ordinary annuity
3.	annuity due
4.	annuities certain
5.	contingent annuities
6.	sinking fund
7.	present value of annuity

Theory Tips (and/or Cautions)

8. The value of an annuity is the value of a series of payments _____ interest.
9. With an ordinary annuity, regular payments (or deposits) are made at the _____ of the period.
10. With an annuity due, regular payments (or deposits) are made at the _____ of the period.
11. What we call _____ _____ in compounding is now called the value of annuity.
12. Ordinary annuities and annuities due both find _____ _____.
13. The _____ _____ will give a higher final value than _____ _____ since money is put in at the beginning of the period.
14. The _____ _____ of an ordinary annuity finds the present worth.
15. In calculating annuity due by the ordinary annuity table, you should add _____ period and subtract _____ payment.
16. Annuity payments do not have to be _____.
17. The sinking fund payment can be checked by the _____ _____ table.
18. In a sinking fund you determine the amount of _____ _____ you need to achieve a financial goal.

8.	plus
9.	end
10.	beginning
11.	maturity value
12.	future value
13.	annuity due; ordinary annuity
14.	present value
15.	one; one
16.	yearly
17.	ordinary annuity
18.	periodic payment

Calculations/Applications

Do calculations on scrap paper as needed. Worked-out solutions are provided at end.

19. Calculate by table the value of an investment after 3 years on an ordinary annuity of $6,000 made semiannually at 6%.
20. Redo your calculation in #19 assuming an annuity due.
21. Nancy Cram won the Boston Lottery and will receive a $5,000 check at the beginning of each 6 months for the next 7 years. If Nancy deposits each check into an account that pays 8%, how much will she have at the end of the 7 years?
22. What must you invest today to receive a $6,000 annuity for 10 years quarterly at 8% annual rate? All withdrawals will be made at the end of each period.
23. Pete O'Sullivan wants to set up a scholarship fund to provide 6 $4,000 scholarships for the next 5 years. If money can be invested at an annual rate of 6%, how much should Pete invest today?

19.	$38,810.40
20.	$39,975
21.	$95,118
22.	$164,132.40
23.	$101,097.60

24. Long Co. issued bonds that will mature to a value of $80,000 in 8 years. Long is setting up a sinking fund. Interest rates are 8% compounded quarterly. What will be the amount of each sinking fund payment? Verify your answer by the amount of annuity. It will be off due to rounding of tables. (Use tables in *Business Math Handbook*.)

Worked-Out Solutions to Calculations/Applications Section

19. $\dfrac{6\%}{2} = 3\%$ 3 yrs. $\times$ 2 = 6 periods

$6,000 $\times$ 6.4684 = $38,810.40

20. 3%, 7 periods
$6,000 $\times$ 7.6625 = $45,975
$$\begin{array}{r} -\ 6,000 \\ \hline \$39,975 \end{array}$$

21. $\dfrac{8\%}{2} = 4\%$ 7 yrs. $\times$ 2 = $\begin{array}{r} 14 \\ +\ 1 \\ \hline 15 \text{ periods} \end{array}$

$5,000 $\times$ 20.0236 = $100,118
$$\begin{array}{r} -\ 5,000 \\ \hline \$\ 95,118 \end{array}$$

22. $\dfrac{8\%}{4} = 2\%$ 10 yrs. $\times$ 4 = 40 periods
$6,000 $\times$ 27.3554 = $164,132.40

23. 6%, 5 periods
$24,000 $\times$ 4.2124 = $101,097.60

24. $\dfrac{8\%}{4} = 2\%$ 8 yrs. $\times$ 4 = 32 periods

$80,000 $\times$ .0226 = $1,808
Verify: $1,808 $\times$ 44.2269 = $79,962 (due to rounding of tables)

Word Problem Practice Quiz

Check with your instructor for complete worked-out solutions.

13–1. Charlie Gold made deposits of $700 at end of each year for 7 years. The interest rate is 7% compounded annually. What is the value of Charlie's annuity at end of 7 years?

13–2. James Will promised to pay his son $500 semiannually for 5 years. Assume James can invest his money at 8% in an ordinary annuity. How much must James invest today to pay his son $500 semiannually for 5 years?

13–3. Bill Martin invests $6,000 at the end of each year for 7 years in an ordinary annuity at 6% interest compounded annually. What is the final value of Bill's investment at the end of year 7?

13–4. Alice Long has decided to invest $400 semiannually for 5 years in an ordinary annuity at 10%. As her financial advisor, could you calculate for Alice the total cash value of the annuity at the end of year 5?

13–5. At the beginning of each period for 5 years, Rob Flynn invests $800 semiannually at 12%. What is the cash value of this annuity due at the end of year 5?

13–6. Murphy Company borrowed money that must be repaid in 5 years. So that the loan will be repaid at end of year 5, the company invests $8,500 at end of each year at 8% interest compounded annually. What was the amount of the original loan?

13–7. Jane Frost wants to receive semiannual payments of $25,000 for 10 years. How much must she deposit at her bank today at a 10% interest rate compounded semiannually?

13–8. Jeff Associates borrowed $70,000. The company plans to set up a sinking fund that will repay the loan at the end of 20 years. Assume a 12% interest rate compounded semiannually. What must Jeff pay into the fund each period? Check your answer by table.

13–9. At the beginning of each period for 7 years, Michael Ring invested $1,200 at 10% interest compounded semiannually. What is the value of this annuity due?

13–10. Jim Green wants to receive $8,000 each year for the next 12 years. Assume an interest rate of 6% compounded annually. How much must Jim invest today?

CHAPTER 14

Self-Paced Worksheet

Cover the answers on the right and fill in each blank. After answering the question, look to the right for your answer.

Vocabulary Review

1. _____ is the process of paying back a loan (principal and interest) by equal periodic payments.
2. Cash price less down payment equals _____ _____.
3. The _____ _____ _____ is the true or effective annual interest rate charged by sellers.
4. The sum of daily balances divided by the number of days in the billing cycle equals the _____ _____ _____.
5. A _____ _____ results when money is borrowed by the holder of a credit card.
6. The total of all payments less actual loan cost equals the _____ _____.
7. The deferred payment price is the total of all monthly payments _____ down payment.
8. Open-end credit is a _____ credit account.
9. The Rule of 78 is one method to compute _____ on consumer finance loans.
10. The _____ is the finance charge a customer receives for paying off a loan early.

1. amortization
2. amount financed
3. annual percentage rate
4. average daily balance
5. cash advance
6. finance charge
7. plus
8. revolving
9. rebates
10. rebate

Theory Tips (and/or Cautions)

11. The finance charge can include the cost of _____ reports, mandatory bank fees, etc.
12. APR can be calculated by using _____.
13. The Truth in Lending Act doesn't dictate what can be _____ for interest.
14. The loan amortization table is per _____. The table is used to calculate the monthly payment.
15. The U.S. Rule applied partial payment to interest _____ and then the remainder of the payment _____ the principal.
16. In calculating the rebate fraction, the _____ represents the sum of digits based on the number of months to go.
17. The denominator of the rebate fraction represents the sum of digits based on the _____ number of months of the loan.
18. Most companies calculate the _____ _____ as a percentage of the average daily balance.
19. A cash advance is a _____ _____ from a credit card company.
20. In calculating the average daily balance, the days of the _____ _____ has to be known to arrive at the final number of days of the current balance.

11. credit
12. tables
13. charged
14. $1,000
15. first; reduces
16. numerator
17. total
18. finance charge
19. cash loan
20. billing cycle

Calculations/Applications

Do calculations on scrap paper as needed. Worked-out solutions are at the end.

21. Gail Sentner bought a new Chevrolet for $16,500, putting down $500 and paying $300 per month for 60 months. Calculate:

   a. Amount financed.
   b. Finance charge.
   c. Deferred payment price.
   d. APR by table. (Use tables in *Business Math Handbook*.)
   e. Monthly payment by formula.

21. a. $16,000
    b. $2,000
    c. $18,500
    d. 4.5%–4.75%
    e. $300

22. Dan Carl is buying a new Welbilt boat for $9,500. Dan puts down $2,000 and is financing the balance at 11% for 60 months. What is his monthly payment (use the loan amortization table)?

22. $163.05

23. From the following, calculate the finance charge rebate and final payoff:

Loan for 12 months; $6,200; end-of-month loan is repaid: 8; monthly payment; $575

24. Paula Franc bought a desk for $900. She pays $100 a month and is charged $3\frac{1}{2}\%$ interest on the unpaid balance. What is Paula's balance outstanding at the end of month 1?

25. Calculate the average daily balance from the following (30-day biling cycle):

7/21	Billing date	Previous balance	$400
7/28	Payment		$ 40 credit
7/31	Charge		$ 60
8/6	Payment		$ 10 credit
8/13	Cash advance		$ 50

Worked-Out Solutions for Calculations/Applications Section

21. **a.** $16,500 - $500 = $16,000

b. $18,000 (60 × $300) − $16,000 = $2,000

c. $18,000 (60 × $300) + $500 = $18,500

d. $\dfrac{\$2,000}{\$16,000} \times \$100 = \$12.5$ between 4.5% and 4.75%

e. $\dfrac{\$2,000 + \$16,000}{60} = \$300$

22. $\dfrac{\$7,500}{\$1,000} = 7.5 \times \$21.74 = \$163.05$

23. **Step 1:**
$$\begin{array}{r} 12 \times \$575 = \$6,900 \\ 8 \times \$575 = \underline{4,600} \\ \$2,300 \end{array}$$

Step 2:
$$\begin{array}{r} 12 \times \$575 = \$6,900 \\ \underline{-6,200} \\ \$\ 700 \end{array}$$

Step 3: 12 − 8 = 4

Step 4: $\dfrac{10}{78}$

Step 5: $\dfrac{10}{78} \times \$700 = \$89.74$

Step 6: $2,300 − $89.74 = $2,210.26

24. $900 × 3.5% = $31.50

$100 − $31.50 = $68.50

$900 − $68.50 = $831.50

25.
$$\begin{array}{rr} 7 \times \$400 & \$\ 2,800 \\ 3 \times \$360 & 1,080 \\ 6 \times \$420 & 2,520 \\ 7 \times \$410 & 2,870 \\ 7 \times \$460 & \underline{3,220} \\ (30 - 23) & \$12,490 \end{array}$$

$\dfrac{\$12,490}{30} = \$416.33$

Word Problem Practice Quiz

Check with your instructor for complete worked-out solutions.

14–1. Andy Troll bought a new delivery truck for $16,000. Andy put a down payment of $3,000 and paid $255 monthly for 60 months. What is the total amount financed and the total finance charge that Andy paid at the end of the 60 months?

14–2. Joan Porl read the following advertisement: Price, $17,000; down payment, $500 cash or trade; amount financed, $16,500; $399 per month for 60 months; finance charge, $7,440; and total payments $23,940.
(1) Check finance charge and (2) calculate the APR by table.

14–3. Barry Crate bought a desk for $7,000. Based on his income, he could only afford to pay back $900 per month. There is a charge of $2\frac{1}{2}$% interest on the unpaid balance. The U.S. Rule is used in the calculation. Could you calculate at the end of month 2 the balance outstanding?

14–4. Tony Jean borrowed $8,150 to travel to Europe to see his son Bill. His loan was to be paid in 48 monthly installments of $198. At the end of 11 months, Tony's daughter Joan convinced him that he should pay off the loan early. What is Tony's rebate and his payoff amount?

14–5. Jim Smith bought a new boat for $9,000. Jim put down $1,000 and financed the balance at 11% for 60 months. What is his monthly payment? Use the Loan Amortization table.

14–6. Al Rolf bought an air conditioner with $150 down and 38 equal monthly installments of $35. The total purchase price (cash price) of the air conditioner was $1,050. Al decided to pay off the bill after the 30th payment. What is Al

entitled to as a rebate on the finance charge? What will Al's payoff be?

14–7. Joanne Flynn bought a new boat for $15,000. She put a $2,000 down payment on the boat. The bank's loan was for 48 months. Finance charges totaled $4,499.84. Assume Joanne decides to pay off the loan at the end of the 26th month. What rebate would she be entitled to and what is the actual payoff amount? Round monthly payment to nearest cent.

14–8. Calculate APR by table for the following advertisement:
$98.50 per month; cash price, $2,899; down payment $199, cash or trade; 36 months with bank approved credit, amount financed, $2,700; finance charge, $846; total payments, $3,546.

14–9. From the following facts, Bill Jess has requested you to caculate the average daily balance:

30-day billing cycle

3/18	Billing date	Previous balance	$880
3/24	Payment		70
3/29	Charge		350
4/5	Payment		30
4/9	Charge		400

14–10. Glen James borrowed $7,200 from Able Loan Company. The loan is to be repaid in 48 monthly installments of $199. At the end of 14 months, Glen decided to pay off the loan. What is Glen's rebate and payoff amount?

CHAPTER 15

Self-Paced Worksheet

Cover the answers on the right and fill in each blank. After answering the question, look to the right for your answer.

Vocabulary Review

1. The rate for an _____ _____ mortgage is lower than a fixed rate mortgage.
2. The _____ _____ shows how each monthly payment is broken down into interest and principal reduction.
3. A _____ mortgage is paid every two weeks rather than monthly.
4. A _____ _____ loan provides a cheap and readily accessible line of credit backed by equity in your home.
5. A _____ is a one-time payment made at closing.
6. A _____ is the cost of home less the down payment.
7. A special account set up to protect the bank is called an _____ account.
8. In a _____ _____ mortgage, the borrower pays less at the beginning of the mortgage. As years go on, the payment increases.
9. When property passes from the seller to the buyer, _____ _____ may include credit reports, recording costs, lawyer's fees, points, title search, etc.

1.	adjustable rate
2.	amortization schedule
3.	biweekly
4.	home equity
5.	point
6.	mortgage
7.	escrow
8.	graduated payment
9.	closing costs

Theory Tips (and/or Cautions)

10. In a 30-year fixed mortgage, you are locked in to the interest rate, unless you _____ to get a lower interest rate.
11. In a 15-year fixed rate mortgage you need a larger down payment. The monthly payment will be _____.
12. A graduated-payment may have _____ APR than fixed or variable rates.
13. The _____ _____ requires 26 biweekly payments a year. It shortens the term loan and saves a substantial amount of interest.
14. Home equity loans are _____ deductible.
15. Points are a _____ charge that is a percent of the mortgage.
16. A rise in _____ rates could cost a home buyer thousands of extra dollars in interest cost over the life of a mortgage.
17. In the early payments of a mortgage, most of the monthly payment goes to cover _____ with a smaller reduction in _____.
18. If you plan to own your home for a short time _____ may not be an attractive alternative to get a lower rate of interest.

10.	refinance
11.	higher
12.	higher
13.	biweekly mortgage
14.	tax
15.	one-time
16.	interest
17.	interest; principal
18.	refinancing

Calculations/Applications

Do calculations on scrap paper as needed. Worked-out solutions are provided at end.

19. Twila Griffen bought a new condominium for $110,000. She put down 10% and obtained a mortgage at 8% for 25 years. What is her (a) monthly payment, (b) the total interest cost, and (c) cost of interest for the first payment?
20. Alison Wolfe bought a new chalet for $80,000 at 9% for 30 years. Prepare an amortization schedule for the first two periods.

21. Aster Smith bought a home in Ventura, California for $110,000. He put down 20% and obtained a mortgage for 30 years at 10%. (a) What is Aster's monthly payment? (b) What is the total interest cost of the loan?
22. If in Problem #21 the rate of interest is 12%, what is the difference in interest cost?

19.	a.	$764.28
	b.	$130,284
	c.	$660
20.	1.	$600, $44 $79,956
	2.	$599.67, $44.33 $79,911.67
21.	a.	$772.64
	b.	$190,150.40
22.		$47,836.80

19. $\dfrac{\$99,000}{\$1,000} = 99 \times \$7.72 = \$764.28$

$300 \times \$764.28 = \$229,284$

$\qquad\qquad\qquad\quad - \ 99,000$

$\qquad\qquad\qquad\quad \overline{\$130,284}$

$\$99,000 \times .08 \times \dfrac{1}{12} = \$660$

Note:

$\qquad 12 \times 25 \text{ years} = 300 \text{ payments}$

20. $\dfrac{\$80,000}{\$1,000} = 80 \times \$8.05 = \$644$

Payment	Principal	Interest	Principal reduction	Balance of principal
1	$80,000	$600	$44	$79,956
		$\left(\$80,000 \times .09 \times \dfrac{1}{12}\right)$		
2	$79,956	$599.67	$44.33	$79,911.67
		$\left(\$79,956 \times .09 \times \dfrac{1}{12}\right)$		

21. $\dfrac{\$88,000}{\$1,000} = 88 \times \$8.78 = \$772.64$

$360 \times \$772.64 = \$278,150.40$

$\qquad\qquad\qquad\quad - \ 88,000.00$

$\qquad\qquad\qquad\quad \overline{\$190,150.40}$

22. $\ \ 88 \times \$10.29 \ = \$\quad\ \ 905.52$

$360 \times \$905.52 = \quad 325,987.20$

$\qquad\qquad\qquad\quad - \ \ 88,000.00$

$\qquad\qquad\qquad\quad \ \ 237,987.20$

$\qquad\qquad\qquad\quad -190,150.40$

$\qquad\qquad\qquad\quad \overline{\$\ \ \ 47,836.80}$

Word Problem Practice Quiz

Check with your instructor for complete worked-out solutions.

15–1. Jeff Jones purchased a new condominium for $129,000. The bank required a $30,000 down payment. Assume a rate of 10% on a 25-year mortgage. What is Jeff's monthly payment and total interest cost?

15–2. Bill Allen bought a home in Arlington, Texas, for $118,000. He put down 30% and obtained a mortgage for 30 years at 11%. What is Bill's monthly payment? What is the total interest cost of the loan?

15–3. Jim Smith took out a $60,000 mortgage on a ski chalet. The bank charged 3 points at closing. What did the points cost Jim in dollars?

15–4. Bill Jones bought a new split-level home for $190,000 with 20% down. He decided to use Victory Bank for his mortgage. They were offering $11\frac{3}{4}\%$ for 25-year mortgages. Could you provide Bill with an amortization schedule for the first month?

15–5. Janet Fence bought a home for $215,000 with a down payment of $50,000. The interest rate was $10\frac{1}{2}\%$ for 35 years. Calculate Janet's payment per $1,000 and her monthly mortgage payment.

15–6. Marvin Bass bought a home for $170,000 with a down payment of $20,000. His rate of interest is $11\frac{1}{2}\%$ for 25 years. Calculate Marvin's payment per $1,000 and his monthly mortgage payment.

15–7. Using Problem 15–6, calculate the total cost of interest for Marvin Bass.

15–8. Marsha Terban bought a home for $200,000 with a down payment of $40,000. Her rate of interest is 12% for 35 years. Calculate her (1) monthly payment, (2) first payment broken down into interest and principal, and (3) balance of mortgage at the end of the month.

15–9. Tom Burke bought a home in Virginia for $135,000. He puts down 20% and obtains a mortgage for 25 years at $12\frac{1}{2}$%. What is Tom's monthly payment and the total interest cost of the loan?

15–10. Susan Lake is concerned about the financing of a home. She saw a small cottage that sells for $60,000. If she puts 20% down, what will her monthly payment be at (1) 25 years, 10%; (2) 25 years, 11%; (3) 25 years, 12%; and (4) 25 years, 13%? What is the total cost of interest over the cost of the loan for each assumption?

CHAPTER 16

Self-Paced Worksheet

Cover the answers on the right and fill in each blank. After answering the question, look to the right for your answer.

Vocabulary Review

1. _____ represents the owner's investment in a sole proprietorship.
2. The _____ _____ is a financial report that lists assets, liabilities, and equity.
3. Things of value owned by a business are called _____.
4. The owner's equity of a corporation is called _____ _____.
5. _____ _____ is the amount of a corporation's earnings that the company retains in the business, not necessarily in cash form.
6. _____ _____ is a method of analyzing financial reports where each amount is compared to one total.
7. _____ _____ is a method of analyzing financial reports where each amount in this period is compared by amount and/or percent to same amount in the last period.
8. _____ _____ is equal to gross sales less sales discounts less sales returns and allowances.
9. Gross profit less operating expenses equals _____ _____.
10. _____ _____ involves analyzing each number as a percentage of a base year.
11. Current ratio is current assets divided by _____ _____.
12. _____ _____ is net sales divided by total assets.
13. _____ _____ is the relationship of one number to another.
14. Savings received by the buyer for paying for merchandise before a certain date are called _____ _____.

Theory Tips (and/or Cautions)

15. Capital does not mean _____.
16. Capital is not found in the _____ _____.
17. Current assets are consumed or converted into cash within _____ _____.
18. Companies use _____ and _____ assets in their business operation rather than for resale.
19. Land is an asset that doesn't _____.
20. Current liabilities are obligations that must be paid within _____ year.
21. Horizontal analysis needs comparative columns because we take the difference _____ periods of time.
22. The _____ _____ is a financial report that is prepared for a specific period of time.
23. The _____ _____ _____ _____ doesn't represent the selling price of goods sold by companies. It represents the cost of bringing the goods into the company.
24. Sales discounts are not the same as _____ discounts.
25. The base year in trend analysis is assumed to be _____ percent.
26. In the ACID test calculation, _____ and _____ expenses are subtracted.
27. The _____ _____ ratio analyzes if assets are being utilized efficiently.
28. Many companies compare their ratio analysis to _____ standard.

1. capital
2. balance sheet
3. assets
4. stockholders' equity
5. retained earnings
6. vertical analysis
7. horizontal analysis
8. net sales
9. net income
10. trend analysis
11. current liabilities
12. asset turnover
13. ratio analysis
14. purchase discounts

15. cash
16. stockholders' equity
17. one year
18. plant; equipment
19. depreciate
20. one
21. between
22. income statement
23. cost of merchandise sold
24. trade
25. 100
26. inventory; prepaid
27. asset turnover
28. industry

Calculations/Applications

Do calculations on scrap paper as needed. Worked-out solutions are provided at end.

29. For Moore Corporation, calculate total stockholders' equity from the following: Cash, $8,000; land, $16,000; common stock, $18,000; accounts payable, $4,000; retained earnings, $6,000.

30. Complete vertical analysis (round to the nearest hundredth percent):

	2008	%	2009	%
Current assets:				
Cash	$ 15,000	A.	$ 18,000	D.
Accounts receivable	13,000	B.	5,000	E.
Merchandise inventory	42,000	C.	9,000	F.
Total current assets	$150,000		$120,000	

31. From the following information, calculate:
   a. net sales; b. cost of merchandise (goods) sold; c. gross profit from sales; d. net income.

   Gross sales, $42,000; sales returns and allowances, $4,000; beginning inventory, $8,000; net purchases, $9,000; ending inventory, $6,200; operating expenses, $8,400.

32. Prepare a trend analysis from the following, assuming a base year of 2006. Round to the nearest whole percent.

	2009	2008	2007	2006
Sales	$39,000	$65,000	$31,000	$40,000

33. Given: Total current assets, $20,000; accounts receivable, $8,000; total current liabilities, $12,000; inventory, $6,000; net sales, $40,000; total assets, $37,000; net income $8,400.
   Calculate:
   a. Current ratio (to nearest hundredth).
   b. Acid test (to nearest hundredth).
   c. Average day's collection.
   d. Profit margin on sales.

Answers column:

29. $24,000

30. A. 10%
    B. 8.67%
    C. 28%
    D. 15%
    E. 4.17%
    F. 7.5%

31. a. $38,000
    b. $10,800
    c. $27,200
    d. $18,800

32. 1999: 100%
    2000: 78%
    2001: 163%
    2002: 98%

33. a. 1.67
    b. 1.17
    c. 72 days
    d. 21%

Worked-Out Solutions to Calculations/Applications Section

29. $18,000 + $6,000 = $24,000

30. A. $\frac{\$15,000}{\$150,000} = 10\%$ D. $\frac{\$18,000}{\$120,000} = 15\%$

    B. $\frac{\$13,000}{\$150,000} = 8.67\%$ E. $\frac{\$5,000}{\$120,000} = 4.17\%$

    C. $\frac{\$42,000}{\$150,000} = 28\%$ F. $\frac{\$9,000}{\$120,000} = 7.5\%$

31. a. $42,000 − $4,000 = $38,000
    b. $8,000 + $9,000 − $6,200 = $10,800
    c. $38,000 − $10,800 = $27,200
    d. $27,200 − $8,400 = $18,800

32.

2009	2008	2007	2006
98%	163%	78%	100%
$\left(\frac{\$39,000}{\$40,000}\right)$	$\left(\frac{\$65,000}{\$40,000}\right)$	$\left(\frac{\$31,000}{\$40,000}\right)$	

33. a. $\frac{\$20,000}{\$12,000} = 1.67$ b. $\frac{\$20,000 - \$6,000}{\$12,000} = 1.17$

    c. $\frac{\dfrac{\$8,000}{\$40,000}}{360} = 72 \text{ days}$ d. $\frac{\$8,400}{\$40,000} = 21\%$

Word Problem Practice Quiz

Check with your instructor for complete worked-out solutions.

16-1. The total debt to total assets of the Jones Company was .91. The total of Jones' assets was $500,000. What is the amount of total debt to Jones Company?

16-2. Beaver Company has a current ratio of 1.88. The acid-test ratio is 1.61. The current liabilities of Beaver are $42,000. Could you calculate the dollar amount of merchandise inventory? Assume no prepaid expenses.

16-3. The asset turnover of River Company is 5.1. The total assets of River are $89,000. What are River's net sales?

16-4. Jangles Corporation has earned $79,000 after tax. The accountant calculated the return on equity as .14. What was Jangles Corporation's stockholders' equity?

16-5. In analyzing the income statement of Ryan Compay, cost of goods sold has decreased from 2003 to 2009 by 5.1%. The cost of goods sold was $15,900 in 2009. What was the cost of goods sold in 2008?

16-6. Don Williams received a memo requesting that he complete a trend analysis of the following using 2008 as the base year and rounding each percent to the nearest whole percent. Could you help Don with the request?*

Sales	$440,000	$410,000	390,000	$400,000
Gross profit	180,000	200,000	240,000	250,000
Net income	$260,000	$210,000	$150,000	$150,000

*We assume no operating expenses.

16-7. Bill Barnes has requested that you calculate the asset turnover from the following (round answer to nearest tenth):

Gross sales	$55,000
Sales discount	$3,000
Sales returns and allowances	$2,000
Total assets	$34,000

16-8. Al Bean has requested you to calculate the cost of merchandise sold from the following: Sales, $52,000; beginning inventory, $2,800; purchases, $21,500; purchase discounts, $200; and ending inventory, $6,100.

16-9. The bookkeeper of Flynn Company has requested you to calculate the company's gross profit, based on the following: Sales, $28,100; sales returns and allowances $3,000; operating expenses, $5,100; beginning inventory, $700; net purchases, $9,000; and ending inventory, $1,200.

16-10. John's Pizza has an asset turnover of 2.8. The total assets were $80,000. What were the net sales of John's Pizza?

CHAPTER 17

Self-Paced Worksheet

Cover the answers on the right and fill in each blank. After answering the question, look to the right for your answer.

Vocabulary Review

1. Cost less accumulated depreciation equals _____ _____.
2. _____ is the process of allocating the cost of an asset (less residual value) over the asset's estimated life.
3. A table showing the amount of depreciation expense, accumulated depreciation, and book value for each period of time for a plant asset is called a _____ _____.
4. _____ value is the estimated value of a plant asset after depreciation is taken (or end of useful life).
5. _____ _____ is the amount of depreciation that has accumulated on plant and equipment assets.
6. The estimated number of years the plant asset is used is called its _____ _____.
7. _____ method of depreciation spreads an equal amount of depreciation each year over the life of the asset.

1.	book value
2.	depreciation
3.	depreciation schedule
4.	residual (salvage)
5.	accumulated depreciation
6.	useful life
7.	straight-line

Theory Tips (and/or Cautions)

8. _____ _____ cannot be less than residual value.
9. _____ can be indirect tax savings for the company.
10. Companies cannot depreciate _____.
11. Companies do not take the full month's depreciation for assets bought after the _____ of the month.
12. Units-of-production method is based on _____ rather than passage of time.
13. The denominator of the fraction in the sum-of-the-years'-digits calculation remains the _____ for each calculation.
14. In the declining-balance method, you cannot depreciate below the _____ value.
15. To calculate depreciation expense in the declining-balance method, multiply the _____ _____ of equipment at _____ of year times depreciation rate.
16. In the declining-balance method, _____ _____ was not subtracted in the calculation.
17. MACRS is how a company records depreciation for _____ purposes.

8.	book value
9.	depreciation
10.	land
11.	15th
12.	usage
13.	same
14.	residual
15.	book value; beginning
16.	residual value
17.	tax

Calculations/Applications

Do calculations on scrap paper as needed. Worked-out solutions are provided at end.

18. Given the following, calculate the yearly depreciation expense using the straight-line method.

    Truck, $30,000; residual value, $5,000; estimated useful life, 5 years.

19. On January 1, Lyon Co. bought a machine for $50,000 with an estimated life of 8 years. The residual value of the machine is $10,000. This machine is expected over its useful life to produce 60,000 units. This machine is expected to produce 9,000 units the first year and 16,000 in year 2. Calculate the depreciation expense for the machine in years 1 and 2.

20. Using MACRS, what would be the first year's depreciation for a waste water sewer plant that cost $700,000?

18.	$5,000 per year
19.	Year 1: $6,030 Year 2: $10,720
20.	$35,000

Worked-Out Solutions to Calculations/Applications Section

18. $\dfrac{\$30,000 - \$5,000}{5 \text{ years}} = \dfrac{\$25,000}{5} = \$5,000$

19. $\dfrac{\$50,000 - \$10,000}{60,000} = \dfrac{\$40,000}{60,000} = \$.67$

   Year 1: $9,000 \times \$.67 = \$6,030$
   Year 2: $16,000 \times \$.67 = \$10,720$

20. $\$700,000 \times .05 = \$35,000$

Word Problem Practice Quiz

Check with your instructor for complete worked-out solutions.

17–1. Alvin Ross bought a truck for $7,000 with an estimated life of 4 years. The residual value of the truck is $1,000. Assume a straight-line method of depreciation. What will be the book value of the truck at the end of year 2? If the truck was bought on September 5, how much depreciation would be taken in year 1?

17–2. Jim Company bought a machine for $5,000 with an estimated life of 5 years. The residual value of the machine is $500. Calculate the (1) annual depreciation and (2) book value at the end of year 3. Assume straight-line depreciation.

17–3. Using Problem 17–2, calculate the first two years' depreciation assuming the units-of-production method. This machine is expected to produce 5,000 units. In year 1, it produced 2,400 units; in year 2, 2,600 units.

17–4. Using Problem 17–2, calculate the first two years' depreciation assuming Jim Company used the declining-balance method at twice the straight-line rate.

17–5. Able Corporation bought a car for $6,750 with an estimated life of 7 years. The residual value of the car is $450. After 2 years, the car was sold for $5,200. What was the difference between the book value and the amount received from selling the car if Able used the straight-line method of depreciation?

17–6. Jerry Jeves bought a new delivery truck for $6,800. The truck had an estimated life of 6 years and a residual value of $500. Prepare a depreciation schedule for the sum-of-the-years'-digits method.

17–7. Marika Katz, owner of Katz Ice Cream, is discussing with her accountant which method of depreciation would be best for her ice cream truck. The cost of the truck was $10,200, with an estimated life of 5 years. The residual value

17–8. Morris Sullivan bought a machine for $6,900. Its estimated life is 5 years, with a $600 residual value. Using MACRS, calculate the depreciation expense per year for this machine over the first 3 years.

CHAPTER 18

Self-Paced Worksheet

Cover the answers on the right and fill in each blank. After answering the question look to the right for your answer.

Vocabulary Review

1. The last-in, first-out method (LIFO) assumes that the _____ inventory brought into the store will be the first sold.

2. The _____ _____ is an inventory method that estimates the cost of ending inventory by using a cost ratio.

3. _____ _____ is the total of all inventories divided by the number of times inventory was taken.

4. _____ _____ is a ratio that indicates how quickly inventory turns.

5. In a _____ inventory system, the inventory records are continually updated.

6. In a _____ inventory system, a physical count of inventory is taken at the end of a time period.

7. The _____ _____ method calculates the cost of ending inventory is taken by identifying each item remaining to the invoice price.

8. _____ expenses are not directly associated with a specific department or product.

9. The _____ _____ _____ uses the cost percentage to calculate the estimated cost of goods sold.

1.	last
2.	retail method
3.	average inventory
4.	inventory turnover
5.	perpetual
6.	periodic
7.	specific identification
8.	overhead
9.	gross profit method

Theory Tips (and/or Cautions)

10. Companies that sell high cost items usually use the _____ _____ method of inventory valuation.

11. Companies with homogeneous products like fuels and grains may use the _____-_____ _____.

12. Cost of goods available for sale less cost of ending inventory equals _____ _____ _____ _____.

13. The cost flow assumption of FIFO or LIFO may or may not exist in the actual _____ flow of goods.

14. During inflation _____ produces a higher income than other inventory methods.

15. FIFO assumes that the first goods brought into the store are the _____ goods sold.

16. The retail method does not require that a company calculate an _____ cost for each item.

17. To use the _____ _____ method, the company must keep track of the average gross profit rate.

18. The inventory turnover at _____ is usually lower than the inventory turnover at _____.

19. A _____ inventory turnover might mean insufficient amounts of inventory resulting in stockouts.

20. The two common methods of calculating the distribution of overhead are by _____ _____ or _____ _____.

10.	specific identification
11.	weighted-average method
12.	cost of goods sold
13.	physical
14.	FIFO
15.	first
16.	inventory
17.	gross profit
18.	retail; cost
19.	high
20.	floor space; sales volume

Calculations/Applications

Do your work on scrap paper as needed. Worked-out solutions are provided at end.

21. From the following calculate by the weighted-average method (a) the cost of ending inventory, and (b), the cost of goods sold. Ending inventory shows 18 units.

21.	**a.** $66.24
	b. $139.76

	Number purchased for resale	Cost per unit	Total
January 1 inventory	12	$2	$24
March 1	9	$3	$27
April 1	20	$4	$80
November 1	15	$5	$75

22. Rework #21 using the FIFO assumption.

23. Rework #21 using the LIFO assumption.

24. Bill's Dress Shop's inventory at cost on January 1 was $32,500. Its retail value is $50,000. During the year, Bill purchased additional merchandise at a cost of $170,000 with a retail value of $366,000. The net sales at retail for the year was $345,000. Calculate Bill's inventory at cost by the retail method. Round the cost ratio to the nearest whole percent.

25. On January 1, Font Company had inventory costing $65,000 and during January had net purchases of $118,000. Over recent years, Font's gross profit has averaged 45% on sales. Given that the company has net sales of $190,000, calculate the estimated cost of ending inventory using the gross profit method.

22. a. $87
    b. $119

23. a. $42
    b. $164

24. $34,790

25. $78,500

Worked-Out Solutions to Calculations/Applications Section

21. $\$24 + \$27 + \$80 + \$75 = \dfrac{\$206}{56} = \$3.68$

$18 \times \$3.68 = \$66.24$ cost of ending inventory
$\$206 - \$66.24 = \$139.76$ cost of goods sold

22. $15 \times \$5 = \$75$
$3 \times \$4 = \underline{12}$
$\$87$ cost of ending inventory
$\$206 - \$87 = \$119$ cost of goods sold

23. $12 \times \$2 = \$24$
$6 \times \$3 = \underline{18}$
$\$42$ cost of ending inventory
$\$206 - \$42 = \$164$ cost of goods sold

24.

	Cost	Retail
Beginning inventory	$ 32,500	$ 50,000
Purchases	170,000	366,000
Cost of goods available for sale	$202,500	$416,000
Less net sales for the year		345,000
Ending inventory at retail		$ 71,000
Cost ratio $\dfrac{\$202,500}{\$416,000} = 49\%$		49%
Ending inventory at cost		$ 34,790

25.

Inventory, January 1	$ 65,000
Net purchases	118,000
Cost of goods available for sale	$183,000
Less: Estimated cost of goods sold:	
Net sales at retail $190,000	
Cost percentage (100% − 45%) .55	
Estimated cost of goods sold	$104,500
Estimated inventory, January 31	$ 78,500

Word Problem Practice Quiz

Check with your instructor for complete worked-out solutions.

18–1. Marvin Company has a beginning inventory of 7 sets of paints at a cost of $1.75 each. During the year, the store purchased 3 at $1.80, 7 at $2.50, 5 at $2.75, and 10 at $3.00. By the end of the year, 19 sets were sold. Calculate (1) the number of paint sets in stock and (2) the cost of ending inventory under LIFO.

18–2. Calculate the cost of ending inventory under FIFO for Problem 18–1. Round to nearest cent the average cost per unit before calculating the cost of ending inventory.

18–3. Calculate the cost of ending inventory by weighted average for Problem 18–1. Round to nearest cent the average cost per unit before calculating cost of ending inventory.

18–4. Jeffrey Company allocated overhead expenses to all departments on the basis of floor space (square feet) occupied by each department. The total overhead expenses for a recent year amounted to $90,000. Department A occupied 15,000 square feet; Department B, 5,000 square feet; Department C, 9,500 square feet. What is the amount of the overhead allocated to Department C? Round ratio to nearest whole percent.

18–5. In Problem 18–4, what amount of overhead is allocated to Department A? Round ratio to nearest percent.

18–6. Moose Company has a beginning inventory at a cost of $78,000 and an ending inventory costing $86,000. Sales were $410,000. Assume Moose's markup rate is 31%. Based on the selling price what is the inventory turnover at cost? Round to nearest hundredth.

18–7. May's Dress Shop's inventory at cost on January 1 was $38,500. Its retail value is $61,000. During the year, May purchased additional merchandise at a cost of $188,000 with a retail value of $402,000. The net sales at retail for the year was $352,000. Could you calculate May's inventory at cost by the retail method? Round cost ratio to nearest whole percent.

18–8. A sneaker shop has made the following wholesale purchases of new running shoes: 15 pairs at $26, 24 pairs at $27.50, and 8 pairs at $33.00. An inventory taken last week indicates that 17 pairs are still in stock. Calculate the cost of this inventory by FIFO.

18–9. The manager of Saikes Department Store is having difficulty calculating the inventory turnover at retail. The beginning retail inventory was $88,000 and the ending retail inventory was $96,000. The store's net sales were $715,000 and the cost of goods was $492,000. Assist the manager by computing the turnover to the nearest hundredth.

18–10. Over the past five years, the gross profit rate for Jerome Corp. wsa 42%. Using the gross profit method, estimate the cost of ending inventory given the following: Beginning inventory, $7,000; net purchases, $70,000; net sales at retail, $58,000.

CHAPTER 19

Self-Paced Worksheet

Cover the answers on the right and fill in each blank. After answering the question, look to the right for your answer.

Vocabulary Review

1. _____ _____ is the value of a property that an assessor sets that is used in calculating property taxes.
2. _____ _____ is a tax on specific luxury items or nonessentials.
3. A _____ is $\frac{1}{10}$ of a cent of $\frac{1}{1,000}$ of a dollar.
4. _____ _____ is a tax levied on consumers for certain sales of merchandise or services by states, counties, or various local governments.
5. _____ _____ is a tax that raises revenue for school districts, cities, counties, and the like.
6. Cars, home, furnishings, and jewelry are examples of _____ _____.
7. Land, buildings, and so on are examples of _____ _____.

1. assessed value
2. excise tax
3. mill
4. sales tax
5. property tax
6. personal property
7. real property

Theory Tips (and/or Cautions)

8. The list of items that is taxed for sales tax will _____ from state to state.
9. Trade discounts are subtracted from the _____ _____ before sales tax is computed.
10. The cost of shipping, handling, and so on are _____ subject to sales tax.
11. Sellers also take cash discounts on the _____ _____ before adding the sales tax.
12. _____ _____ is often calculated as a percentage of the selling price, although the tax can be stated as a fixed amount per item sold.
13. Real property and personal property are both subject to _____ _____.
14. In determining the tax rate, it should be _____ _____ to the indicated digit, even if it is less than 5.
15. To represent the number of mills as a tax rate per dollar, we divide the tax rate in decimal by _____.
16. In calculating property tax due, the total assessed value represents the _____.
17. In some states, a portion of assessed value is excluded from _____ _____ for senior citizens.

8. vary
9. original price
10. not
11. base price
12. excise tax
13. property tax
14. rounded up
15. .001
16. base
17. property tax

Calculations/Applications

Do calculations on scrap paper as needed. Worked-out solutions are provided at end.

18. John Sullivan, Jr., bought a new Apple computer for $1,900. The price included a 7% sales tax. What is (a) the sales tax and (b) the selling price before the tax?
19. In the community of Rose, the market value of a home is $150,000. The assessment rate is 40%. What is the assessed value?
20. Blooker County needs $910,000 from property tax to meet its budget. The total value of assessed property in Blooker is $141,000,000. What is the tax rate of Blooker? Round to the nearest ten thousandth. Express the rate in mills (to one tenth).
21. The home of Wally Waller is assessed at $75,000. The tax rate is 13.51 mills. What is the tax on Wally's home?
22. Lou's warehouse has a market value of $5,000,000. The property in Lou's area is assessed at 40% of the market value. The tax rate is $142.50 per $1,000 of assessed value. What is Lou's property tax?

18. a. $124.30
    b. $1,775.70
19. $60,000
20. 6.5 mills
21. $1,013.25
22. $285,000

Worked-Out Solutions to Calculations/Applications Section

18. $\dfrac{\$1,900}{1.07} = \$1,775.70$

$$\begin{array}{r} \$1,900.00 \\ -1,775.70 \\ \hline \$\ \ 124.30 \end{array}$$

19. $\$150,000 \times .40 = \$60,000$

20. $\dfrac{\$910,000}{\$141,000,000} = .0064539 = .0065$ $\quad \dfrac{.0065}{.001} = 6.5 \text{ mills}$

21. $13.51 \times .001 \times \$75,000 = \$1,013.25$

22. $\$5,000,000 \times .40 = \dfrac{\$2,000,000}{\$1,000} =$

$$\begin{array}{r} 2,000.00 \\ \times\ \$142.50 \\ \hline \$285,000.00 \end{array}$$

Word Problem Practice Quiz

Check with your instructor for complete worked-out solutions.

19–1. Tom Fall bought an $80 fishing rod that is subject to a 6% sales tax and a 12% excise tax. What is the total amount Tom paid for the rod?

19–2. Don Chater bought a new computer for $2,999. This included a 7% sales tax. What is the amount of sales tax and the selling price before the tax?

19–3. Moe Blunt bought a hammer from Jan's Hardware Store for $15.88 plus tax. Jan rang up the sale and looked at her sales tax chart (use table). How much is the total of the sale?

19–4. Sheri Missan bought a ring for $8,000. She must still have to pay a 6% sales tax and an 8% excise tax. The jeweler is shipping the ring so Sheri must also pay a $30 shipping charge. What is the total purchase price of Sheri's ring?

19–5. Al's warehouse has a market value of $175,000. The property in Al's area is assessed at 45% of the market value. The tax rate is $119.20 per $1,000 of assessed value. What is Al's property tax?

19–6. In the community of Ross, the market value of a home is $210,000. The assessment rate is 28%. What is the assessed value?

19–7. Blunt County needs $690,000 from property tax to meet its budget. The total value of assessed property in Blunt is $105,000,000. What is the tax rate of Blunt? Round to nearest hundred thousandths. Express the rate in mills.

19–8. Bill Shass pays a property tax of $3,900. In his community, the tax rate is 47 mills. What is Bill's assessed value to the nearest dollar?

19–9. The home of Bill Burton is assessed at $90,000. The tax rate is 24.60 mills. What is the tax on Bill's home?

19–10. The building of Bill's Hardware is assessed at $118,000. The tax rate is $42.50 per $1,000 of assessed value. What is the tax due?

CHAPTER 20

Self-Paced Worksheet

Cover the answers on the right and fill in each blank. After answering the question, look to the right for your answer.

Vocabulary Review

1. The person(s) designated to receive the face value of the life insurance when the insured dies is called the _____.
2. _____ _____ represents the value of an insurance policy when terminated.
3. Inexpensive life insurance that builds up no cash value is called _____ _____.
4. _____ _____ is an insurance policy that is a combination of term insurance and cash value.
5. When a life insurance policy is terminated, _____ _____ include cash value, additional extended term, and/or additional paid-up.
6. _____ is a type of fire insurance in which the insurer and insured share the risk.
7. _____ represent the amount the insured pays before the insurance company pays.
8. Insurance required by law is called _____ _____.
9. _____ _____ is an optional auto insurance that pays for damages to the auto caused by factors other than from collison (fire, vandalism).
10. The _____ is the insurance company that issues the policy.

1. beneficiary
2. cash value
3. term life
4. 20-year endowment
5. nonforfeiture values
6. coinsurance
7. deductibles
8. compulsory insurance
9. comprehensive insurance
10. insurer

Theory Tips (and/or Cautions)

11. Term insurance has no _____ _____.
12. An insurance company will never pay more than the _____ _____ of a policy.
13. Straight life insurance provides _____ protection.
14. Universal life insurance is basically a _____ _____ insurance plan with flexible premium schedules and benefits.
15. For straight life insurance, the longer the policy is in effect, the _____ the cash value because more premiums have been paid in.
16. In nonforfeiture options, the policy holder could get cash value, reduced paid-up insurance, or _____ _____ _____.
17. Life insurance is per $1,000, while fire insurance is per _____.
18. If the insurance company cancels your fire insurance they cannot use the _____-_____ _____. The result is more of a refund to the policyholder.
19. The bottom of the fraction in the calculation for coinsurance represents the _____ required to meet coinsurance. It is calculated by rate times replacement value.
20. _____ _____ covers injury to other people's autos, trees, buildings, etc.
21. 10/20 means the insurance company will pay damages to people injured or killed by your auto up to _____ for injury to one person per accident or a total of _____ for injuries to two or more people per accident.
22. If the policyholder lowers the deductible for collision comprehensive, an additional _____ results.
23. Premiums for collision, property damage, and comprehensive are not reduced by _____ _____.

11. cash value
12. face value
13. permanent
14. whole life
15. higher
16. extended term insurance
17. $100
18. short-rate table
19. insurance
20. property damage
21. $10,000; $20,000
22. premium
23. no fault

Calculations/Applications

Do calculations on scrap paper as needed. Worked-out solutions are provided at end.

24. Alvin Hersey, age 44, purchased a $90,000, 5-year term life insurance policy. Calculate his annual premium. After 3 years, what is his cash value?
25. Gracie Lantz, age 44, purchased a $80,000 straight life policy. Calculate her annual premium.

24. $405; no cash value
25. $1,224

26. If after 15 years Gracie (problem #25) wants to surrender her policy, what options and what amounts are available to her?

27. Calculate the total annual premium of a building that has an area rating of 1 with a building classification A. The value of the building is $90,000, with contents valued at $40,000.

28. If the insured in problem #27 cancels at the end of month 8, what is the cost of the premium and the refund?

29. If in problem #28 the insurance company cancels at the end of month 8, what is the cost of the premium and the refund?

30. Ring insures a building for $160,000 with 80% coinsurance clause. The replacement value is $400,000. Assume a loss of $90,000 from fire. What will the insurance company pay?

31. Calculate the annual premium of Phil Smool who lives in territory 5 and is a classified driver 18, has a car with age 5 and symbol 2. His state has compulsory insurance and Phil wants to add the following options:

   1. Bodily injury, 500/1000
   2. Damage to someone else's property, 25M
   3. Collision, 100 deductible
   4. Comprehensive, 300 deductible
   5. Towing

26. cash value: $11,840; paid-up, $29,680; extended: 20 yrs., 165 days

27. $392

28. premium: $290.08; refund: $101.92

29. premium: $261.33; refund: $130.67

30. $45,000

31. $865

Worked-Out Solutions to Calculations/Applications Section

24. $\dfrac{\$90,000}{\$1,000} = 90 \times \$4.50 = \$405$

25. $\dfrac{\$80,000}{\$1,000} = 80 \times \$15.30 = \$1,224$

26. Cash value: $80 \times \$148 = \$11,840$
    Paid-up insurance: $80 \times \$371 = \$29,680$
    Extended term: 20 year, 165 days

27. $\dfrac{\$90,000}{\$100}$ $900 \times \$.28 = \$252$

    $\dfrac{\$40,000}{\$100}$ $400 \times \$.35 = \dfrac{\$140}{\$392}$

28. Premium: $\$392 \times \$.74 = \$290.08$
    Refund: $\$392 \times \$.26 = \$101.92$

29. Premium: $\dfrac{8}{12} \times \$392 = \$261.33$

    Refund: $\dfrac{4}{12} \times \$392 = \$130.67$

30. $\dfrac{\$160,000}{\$320,000} = \$.50 \times \$90,000 = \$45,000$

31. **Compulsory**

Bodily	$ 80
Property	$160

   Options

Bodily	$251
Property	$166
Collision	$157 (124 + 33)
Comprehensive	$ 47
Towing	$ 4
Total	$865

Word Problem Practice Quiz

Check with your instructor for complete worked-out solutions.

20–1. Well-known actress Margie Rale, age 44, decided to take out a limited payment life policy. She chose this since she expects her income to decline in future years. Margie decided to take out a 20-year payment life policy with a coverage amount of $70,000. Could you advise Margie of what her annual premium will be? If she decides to stop paying premiums after 10 years, what would be her cash value?

20–2. Joyce Gail has two young children and wants to take out an additional $375,000 of 5-year term insurance. Joyce is 36 years old. What will her additional annual premium be? In 4 years, what cash value would have been built up?

20–3. Roger's office building has a $430,000 value, a rating of 1, and a building classification of A. The contents in the building are valued at $125,000. Could you help Roger calculate his total annual premium?

20–4. Carol Ellen's toy store is worth $50,000 and is insured for $30,000. Assume an 80% coinsurance clause and that a fire caused $150,000 damage. What is the liability of the insurance company?

20–5. Property of Al's Garage is worth $260,000. Al has a fire insurance policy of $200,000 that contains an 80% coinsurance clause. What will the insurance company pay on a fire that causes $108,000 damage?

20–6. Pete Williams had taken out a $69,000 fire insurance policy for his new restaurant at a rate of $.77 per $100. Seven months later, Pete canceled the policy and decided to move his store to a new location. What was the cost of the premium to Pete?

20–7. Earl Miller insured his pizza shop for $200,000 for fire insurance at an annual rate per $100 of $.75. At the end of 10 months, Earl canceled the policy since his pizza shop went out of business. What was the cost of Earl's premium and his refund?

20–8. Ron Tagney insured his real estate office with a fire insurance policy for $88,000 at a cost of $.48 per $100. Eight months later, his insurance company canceled his policy, because of a failure to correct a fire hazard. What did Ron have to pay for the 8 months of coverage? Round to nearest cent.

20–9. Jim Smith, who lives in Territory 5, carries 10/20/5 compulsory liability insurance along with optional collision that has a $500 deductible. Jim was at fault in an accident that caused $3,000 damage to the other auto, and $1,200 damage to his own. Also, the courts awarded $16,000 and $8,000, respectively, to the two passengers in the other car for personal injuries. How much will the insurance company pay, and what is Jim's share of the responsibility?

20–10. Marion Sloan bought a new jeep and insured it with only compulsory insurance 10/20/5. Driving up to her ski chalet one snowy evening, Marion hit a parked van and injured the couple inside. Marion's car had damage of $6,100, and the van she struck had damage of $7,500. After a lengthy court suit, the couple struck were awarded personal injury judgments of $17,000 and $8,100, respectively. What will the insurance company pay for this accident, and what is Marion's responsibility?

CHAPTER 21

Self-Paced Worksheet

Cover the answers on the right and fill in each blank. After answering the questions, look to the right for your answer.

Vocabulary Review

1. A _____ is one who owns stock in a company.

2. A _____ is a written promise by a company that borrows money, usually with fixed-interest payments until maturity (repayment time).

3. A _____ _____ is a cash distribution of the company's profit to owners of stock.

4. An _____ _____ is fewer than 100 shares.

5. The _____-_____ _____ is the closing price per share of stock divided by earnings per share.

6. The _____ _____ _____ is the annual earnings divided by the total number of shares outstanding.

7. _____ represents the distribution of company's profit in cash or stock to owners of stock.

8. _____ _____ _____ result when dividends accumulate when a company fails to pay dividends to cumulative preferred stockholders.

9. A _____ _____ results when a bond sells for less than the face value.

10. A _____ _____ results when a bond sells for more than the face value.

11. The _____ _____ _____ represents the dollar value of one share of a mutual fund.

12. A _____ _____ _____ is a mutual fund that has no sales charge.

1.	stockholder
2.	bond
3.	cash dividend
4.	odd lot
5.	price-earning ratio
6.	earnings per share
7.	dividend
8.	dividends in arrears
9.	bond discount
10.	bond premium
11.	net asset value
12.	no load fund

Theory Tips (and/or Cautions)

13. _____ _____ _____ entitles its owners to a specific amount of dividends in a year. If not paid, these dividends in arrears accumulate.

14. _____ are allowed on the floor of the exchange.

15. _____ are traded in decimals.

16. Bonds are traded in _____ of face amount and not in dollars like stock prices.

17. The _____-_____ _____ does not have one set number. It varies depending on earnings, expectations, economic conditions, etc.

18. A zero PE means the cmopany has _____ earnings.

19. When you buy or sell stock, a _____ charge results.

20. _____ _____ do not have the cumulative feature like preferred stockholders.

21. A bond may sell at a premium if the _____ rate is more attractive than other bonds.

22. The _____ _____ on a bond may be higher than the stated interest rate if one buys the bond at a discount.

23. No matter what _____ you pay for a bond, you will receive yearly interest (face value of bond times yearly interest).

24. For stocks or bonds, _____ close is not listed in today's quotation.

25. For a load fund, the _____ _____ is the NAV plus commission.

26. A front-end load would require the payment of a commission on _____ the shares, while a back-end load will pay the commission when the shares are redeemed.

27. The NAV is the _____ quote per share value.

13.	cumulative preferred stock
14.	stockbrokers
15.	stocks
16.	percent
17.	price-earnings ratio
18.	no
19.	commission
20.	common stockholders
21.	interest
22.	current yield
23.	price
24.	yesterday's
25.	offer price
26.	purchasing
27.	closing

Calculations/Applications

Do calculations on scrap paper as needed. Worked-out solutions are provided at end.

28. Ellen Walters bought 400 shares of IBM stock at $56.25. Assume a commission of 5% of the purchase price. What is the total cost to Ellen?

29. Froll Company earns $6 per share; today the stock is trading at $66. The company pays an annual dividend of $.85. Calculate the (a) price-earning ratio and (b) yield on the stock (to the nearest tenth percent).

30. The stock of Lyon Co. is trading at $62.25. The price-earning ratio is 18 times the earnings. Calculate the earnings per share (to the nearest cent).

31. Alice Disney bought 5 bonds of AUT Company $8\frac{1}{2}06$ at 84 and 7 bonds of QUE Company at $9\frac{3}{4}02$ at 92. Assume the commission on the bonds is $4 per bond. What was the total cost of all purchases?

32. Janice Fall bought one bond for 128. The original bond was $8\frac{1}{4}08$. Calculate the current yield to the nearest tenth percent.

33. Cumulative preferred stockholders receive $.92 per share. There are 80,000 shares. For the last 4 years, no dividends have been paid. This year $280,000 is paid out in dividends. How much dividends to preferred is still in arrears?

34. Lee Winn buys 600 shares of a mutual fund with a NAV of $16.22. This fund has a load charge of 7%. What is the offer price and what did Lee pay for her investment?

28.	$23,625
29.	**a.** 11
	b. 1.3%
30.	$3.46
31.	$10,688
32.	6.4%
33.	$88,000 in arrears
34.	$17.36; $10,416

Worked-Out Solutions to Calculations/Applications Section

28. $400 \times \$56.25 = \$22,500 \times \$1.05 = \$23,625$

29. a. $\dfrac{\$66}{\$6} = 11$ **b.** $\dfrac{\$.85}{\$66} = 1.3\%$

30. $\dfrac{\$62.25}{18} = \$3.46$

31. $5 \times \$840 = \$\ 4,200$
$7 \times \$920 = \underline{\$\ 6,440}$
$\$10,640 + \$48 = \$10,688$

32. $\$1,000 \times .0825 = \$82.50$

$\dfrac{\$82.50}{\$1,280} = 6.4\%$

33. 80,000 shares $\times \$.92 = \$\ 73,600$
$\underline{\times\ 5}$
$\$368,000$
$\underline{280,000}$
$\$\ 88,000$

34. $\$16.22 \times .07 = \$\ 1.14$
$\underline{+\ 16.22}$
$\$17.36$
600 shares $\times \$17.36 = \$10,416$

Word Problem Practice Quiz

Check with your instructor for complete worked-out solutions.

21–1. Norm Dorian bought 600 shares of CBS at $61.25 per share. Assume a commission of 3% of the purchase price. What is the total cost for Norm?

21–2. Assume in Problem 21–1 that Norm sells the stock for $71\frac{1}{8}$ with the same 3% commission rate. What is the bottom line for Norm?

21–3. Jim Corporation pays its cumulative preferred stockholders $2.50 per share. Jim has 40,000 shares of preferred and 80,0000 shares of common stock. In 2004, 2005, and 2006, due to slowdown in the economy, Jim paid no dividends. Now in 2006, the board of directors has decided to pay out $600,000 in dividends. How much of the $600,000 does each class of stock receive as dividends?

21–4. Roger Company earns $5.25 per share. Today the stock is trading at $61\frac{5}{8}$. The company pays an annual dividend of $1.95. Could you calculate the (1) price-earnings ratio (round to nearest whole number) and (2) the yield on the stock (to nearest tenth percent)?

21–5. The stock of VIC Corporation is trading at $70.75. The price-earnings ratio is 14 times earnings. Calculate the earnings per share for VIC Corporation to nearest cent.

21–6. Jerry Ryan bought the 6 bonds of Mort Company. 1106 at 91 and 4 bonds of Inst. System 12 S 09 for 88. If the commission on the bonds is $3.00 per bond, what was the total cost of all the purchases?

21–7. Sue Trenta bought 500 shares of a mutual fund with a NAV of $8.75. This fund has a load charge of 7%. What is (**a**) the offer price and (**b**) what did Sue pay for the investment?

21–8. Ron bought a bond for $88\frac{5}{8}$ of Bee Company. The original bond was $6\frac{3}{4}08$. Ron wanted to know the current yield to nearest tenth percent. Could you help Ron with the calculation?

21–9. Abby Sane decided to buy corporate bonds instead of stock. She desired to have the fixed-interest payments. She purchased 5 bonds of Meg Corporation $8\frac{7}{8}09$ at $89\frac{1}{2}$. As the stockbroker for Abby (assume you charge her a $5 commission per bond), provide her with the following: (1) the total cost of the purchase, (2) total annual interest to be received, and (3) current yield (to nearest tenth percent).

21–10. Mary Blake is considering whether to buy stocks or bonds. She has a good understanding of the pros and cons of both. The stock she is looking at is trading at $60.125, with an annual dividend of $3.65. Meanwhile, the bond is trading at 98 with an annual interest rate of 10%. Could you calculate for Mary her yield (tenth percent) for the stock and the bond, and make appropriate recommendations?

CHAPTER 22

Self-Paced Worksheet

Cover the answers on the right and fill in each blank. After answering the question, look to the right for your answer.

Vocabulary Review

1. A _____ _____ is a visual presentation using horizontal or vertical bars to make comparisons or to show relationships on items of similar makeup.
2. The _____ _____ is the current price divided by the base years price times 100.
3. A _____ _____ shows by table the number of times event(s) occurs.
4. The _____ is a statistical term that represents the central or midpoint of a series of numbers.
5. The _____ is a value that occurs most often in a series of numbers.
6. The _____ is an arithmetic average.
7. _____ _____ are graphical presentations that involve time elements.
8. The _____ _____ is intended to measure the spread of the data about the mean.

1. bar graph
2. price relative
3. frequency distribution
4. median
5. mode
6. mean
7. line graphs
8. standard deviation

Theory Tips (and/or Cautions)

9. When high or low numbers do not significantly affect a list of numbers, the _____ is a good indicator of where the center of the data occurs.
10. If high or low numbers have a significant effect on a list of numbers, the _____ may be better than the mean.
11. The _____ indicates where the center of data occurs without distorting a group of numbers with one or more extreme values.
12. The median in an odd number of values is the _____ value.
13. The median in an even number of values is the _____ of the two middle values.
14. Bar graphs can be _____ or _____.
15. _____ should be of equal size.
16. In a _____ _____ data is spread symmetrically about the mean.

9. mean
10. median
11. median
12. middle
13. average
14. vertical; horizontal
15. intervals
16. normal distribution

Calculations/Applications

Do calculations on scrap paper as needed. Worked-out solutions are provided at end.

17. Sales at Regan Realty totaled six homes for the week. They were as follows: $175,000; $180,000; $150,000; $190,000; $160,000; $90,000. Calculate the (a) mean and (b) median.
18. Computer Village counted the number of customers entering the store for a week. The results were: 1,095; 860; 1,095; 1,111; 865; 888; 1,000. What is the mode?
19. This semester, Dawn Pisai took four 3-credit courses at El Camino College. She received A's in Accounting and Business Math and B's in Logic and Psychology. What is her cumulative grade point average (assume A = 4; B = 3) to the nearest tenth?

17. a. $157,500
    b. $167,500
18. 1,095
19. 3.5

20. Jim's cleaners reported the following sales for the first 10 days of July:

$800	$900
$400	$600
$500	$100
$800	$200
$900	$300

Prepare a frequency distribution.

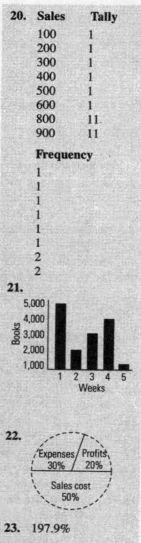

20. Sales	Tally
100	1
200	1
300	1
400	1
500	1
600	1
800	11
900	11

Frequency

1
1
1
1
1
1
2
2

21. Irwin Publishing produced the following number of bound Business Math books during the first 5 weeks of last year:

Week	Bound books
1	5,000
2	2,000
3	3,000
4	4,000
5	1,000

Prepare a bar graph.

21.

22. Kelly Industries reported record profits of 20%. It stated in the report that sales costs were 50% and expenses were 30%. Prepare a pie graph for Kelly.

22.

23. Today, a new Ford Explorer costs $37,000. In 1991, the Explorer cost $18,700. What is the price relative to the nearest tenth percent?

23. 197.9%

24. Calculate the standard deviation of the following data (to nearest hundredth).

2 3 7 13 15

24. 5.83

Worked-Out Solutions to Calculations/Applications Section

17. **a.** $175,000
180,000
150,000
190,000
160,000
90,000
—————
$945,000 ÷ 6 = $157,500

b. ($160,000 + $175,000) ÷ 2 = $167,500

19. 4 × 3 = 12
4 × 3 = 12
3 × 3 = 9 $\frac{42}{12} = 3.5$
3 × 3 = 9
————
42

23. $\frac{37,000}{18,700} = 197.9\%$

118

24.

Data	Data − Mean	(Data − Mean)^2
2	$2 - 8 = -6$	36
3	$3 - 8 = -5$	25
7	$7 - 8 = -1$	1
13	$13 - 8 = 5$	25
15	$15 - 8 = 7$	49
$40 \div 5 = 8$ mean		$136 \div 4 = 34$

$$\sqrt{34} = 5.83$$

Word Problem Practice Quiz

Check with your instructor for complete worked-out solutions.

22–1. The batting averages of the North Shore Community College baseball team's starting 5 are: .333, .285, .395, .250. What is the team's mean batting average?

22–2. The following are the weights of 5 men who enrolled in a fitness class. What is the median weight of the men?

250 lbs.	185 lbs.
290 lbs.	165 lbs.
310 lbs.	

22–3. Today, a new van costs $19,500. In 1980, the van cost $12,000. What is the price relative to the nearest tenth percent?

22–4. Marsha Horton received a quality point average of 3.2 for the semester from State Community College. She received 2 A's, 2 B's, and 1 C. All of her courses were 3 credits and A = 4, B = 3, C = 2, D = 1, and F = 0. Is her grade point average correct?

22–5. Marvin Shoes rang up the following sales for the day: $25, $10, $18, $25, $10, $30, $70, $70, $90, $18, and $25. What is the mode?

22–6. Foxes Gym holds an aerobics class twice a week. The weights of the participants are:

110 lbs.	170 lbs.	150 lbs.
190 lbs.	180 lbs.	130 lbs.
160 lbs.	100 lbs.	120 lbs.
160 lbs.	130 lbs.	110 lbs.
190 lbs.	100 lbs.	130 lbs.
130 lbs.	120 lbs.	140 lbs.

Construct a frequency distribution for Foxes Gym.

22–7. Using the frequency distribution in Problem 22–6, prepare a bar graph.

22–8. Morton's General Store divides its annual sales into categories as follows:

Food	32%
Medical	49%
Services	19%

If a circle graph was prepared, how many degrees would each section be?

22–9. Calculate the standard deviation of the following data to the nearest hundredth.

2   4   8   6   10

22–10. The following are dropout rates for Mr. Ryal's Accounting 1 class for the fall semester of each year:

2002	2003	2004	2005	2006	2007	2008
12%	15%	25%	16%	30%	28%	45%

Construct a line graph from this data.

Calculator Reference Guide

A QUICK REFERENCE GUIDE TO USING YOUR POCKET CALCULATOR*

[+] Plus key to add.
[−] Minus key to subtract.

[×] Multiplication key.
[÷] Dividend key.

[=] Completes calculation.

Topic	Manual example	Using your calculator	Display answer
Addition/subtraction	$15.842 + 3.2 - 24.642$	15.842 [+] 3.2 [−] 24.642 [=]	−5.6
Multiplication/division	$\dfrac{24 \times 26}{12}$	24 [×] 26 [÷] 12 [=]	52
Using a minus sign in multiplication	-14×46	14 [+/−] [×] 46 [=]	−644
Find the portion (using the percent key)	What is 35% of $800?	800 [×] 35 [%] *Note:* No equal sign is punched.	280
Find the rate	$280 is what percent of $800?	280 [÷] 800 [%]	35
Find the base	$280 is 35% of what number?	280 [÷] 35 [%]	800
Discounts	$500 less 5%	500 [−] 5 [%]	475
Adding on sales tax	$600 plus a 5% tax	600 [+] 5 [%]	630
A discount and a tax	$150 less 30% plus a 6% tax	150 [−] 30 [%] [+] 6 [%]	111.30
Simple interest	$1,200 \times 8\% \times \dfrac{60}{365}$	1200 [×] 8 [%] [×] 60 [÷] 365 [=]	15.780821
Using memory	$\dfrac{45}{3 \times 3}$	3 [×] 3 [=] [M +] 45 [÷] [MR] [=]	5
Memory used to solve principal using % key	$\dfrac{\$180}{11.5\% \times \dfrac{30}{360}}$	30 [×] 11.5 [%] [÷] 360 [=] [M+] 180 [÷] [MR][=]	18782.674
Same example without % key	$\dfrac{\$180}{.115 \times \dfrac{30}{360}}$	.115 [×] 30 [÷] 360 [=] [M+] 180 [÷] [MR][=]	18782.674

*Each calculator has variations—check your instruction booklet:

[+/−] Changes sign of number from positive to negative or negative to positive.

[CE] Clears last entry and NOT total.

[MC] Clears memory.

[%] Multiply by percent of the amount.

[M+] Stored in memory (added).

[M−] Subtracted from memory.

[MR] Recalls what is stored in memory.

Reprinted by permission of Texas Instruments Incorporated.

The TI-83 and TI-84 lines of calculators are financial calculators that solve time-value-of-money calculations such as annuities, mortgages, and savings, and generates amortization schedules.

See the Texas Instruments Web site for features http://education.ti.com/educationportal/

SAMPLE QUICK GUIDE REFERENCE

Payment and Compounding Settings (P/Y, C/Y)

The calculators default to 12 payments per year (P/Y) and 12 compounding periods per year (C/Y). You can change one or both of the settings to any number. The examples below assume the calculator is set to four decimal places.

To set both the P/Y and the C/Y to 1:

Press	Display	
2nd [P/Y] 1 ENTER	P/Y =	1.0000
↓	C/Y =	1.0000
2nd [QUIT]		0.0000

The above example shows annual compounding. You may want to set the P/Y to a different number than the C/Y. The following example shows how to set the calculator for a monthly payment that is compounded quarterly.

To set the P/Y to 12 and the C/Y to 4:

Press	Display	
2nd [P/Y] 12 ENTER	P/Y =	12.0000
↓	C/Y =	12.0000
4 ENTER	C/Y =	4.0000
2nd [QUIT]		0.0000

The P/Y and C/Y settings continue indefinitely (even though the calculator is turned off and on), until you change them.

To calculate the future value of a dollar:

What is the future value of $1.00 invested for five years at an interest rate of 7% compounded annually? For this example, set P/Y and C/Y to 1.

Press	Display	
2nd [CLR TVM]		0.0000
1 +/− PV	PV =	−1.0000
5 N	N =	5.0000
7 I/Y	I/Y =	7.0000
CPT FV	FV =	1.4026

Clearing the Calculator

Clearing the calculator is different from resetting it. You can clear one or more values while retaining other data, whereas resetting the calculator clears all data and restores all settings to factory defaults.

To clear the calculator:

Press	To clear
→	One character at a time (including decimal points)
CE/C	An incorrect entry, an error condition, or error message
2nd [QUIT]	All pending operations in standard-calculator mode — or — Out of a prompted worksheet and return to standard-calculator mode (values previously entered remain in the prompted worksheet)
CE/C CE/C	An unfinished calculation — or — A keyed, but not yet entered, variable value in a prompted worksheet — or — Out of a prompted worksheet and return to standard-calculator mode (values previously entered remain in the prompted worksheet)
CE/C 2nd [CLR TVM]	All values (N, I/Y, PV, PMT, FV) in the TVM (Time-Value-of-Money) worksheet
2nd [CLR Work]*	A prompted worksheet (other than TVM) Also returns you to the first variable in the worksheet
2nd [MEM] 2nd [CLR Work]*	All values stored in all 10 memories
O STO and the key for the number of the memory (0–9)	One memory

*You must be in the worksheet you want to clear before using 2nd [CLR Work].

Notes

Notes